How to Make Money from Antiques

For Lou de Swart, a friend in deed

How to Make Money from Antiques

MEL LEWIS

BLANDFORD PRESS
Poole   Dorset

First published in the U.K. 1981 by
Blandford Press Ltd,
Link House, West Street,
Poole, Dorset, BH15 1LL

Copyright © *1981 Mel Lewis*

British Library Cataloguing in Publication Data

Lewis, Mel
  How to make money from antiques.
  1. Antique dealers — Great Britain
  I. Title
  381′.457451′068   NK1110

ISBN 0 7137 1084 5

Typeset and printed by
Permanent Typesetting & Printing Co., Ltd.,
Hong Kong.

Contents

v

Acknowledgements

Special thanks to Jacqueline Pressman, Danny Posner, Bennie Gray, Michael Davis, Bryan Catley, Patrick Gould, Christopher Bangs, J.V. Jenkins Esq., Nick Challon, Annette Phillips, John Jenkins, Kathleen Wowk, Cecil Williamson, Wilfred Beeching, Anthony Irving, James Cartland, David Allison, Editor Hazel Thompson and the staff of *Art & Antiques Weekly* magazine, Fiona Ford, Peter Johnson, Marilyn Kramer — and most especially Jane Kerin, Christie's South Kensington's long-suffering and generously helpful Press officer. Thanks, too, to my personal assistant Gill Colver, who nursed me through many a vocal tantrum and subbed, subtly, through many a written one.

Photographs, unless otherwise stated, appear by courtesy of the author.

Introduction

The more that is known about antiques and collectables (a collectable could have been made yesterday), the more the mystique seems to grow. Have you ever noticed, for example, how it is that in films set in Jacobean times the oak furniture is meticulously researched; only genuine pieces are used and the decor is accurate — or so it seems. The mistake is that age and polish-patinated oak that collectors covet today would not have looked thus in Jacobean times. To be accurate, new furniture should be made in the old style — and it should look *new*.

Almost everyone these days reckons they 'know a thing or two' about antiques. Many already dabble in the market, or would love to, if only they knew how to get started. This book will tell you how.

Certain dealers resist the influx of new faces, especially the competition from part-timers (those who have bread-winning occupations but run a stall at weekend markets) and the like. Nevertheless, surely the more people there are in the trade the better — especially, as dealers constantly claim, as the bulk of business is done inside the trade, dealer buying from and selling to dealer. Competition is healthy in any business — it encourages ingenuity and greater learning. For this reason, Chapter 3 on 'The Importance of Knowledge' is one of the key chapters in this book.

Like many another 'how to' book, this volume should be judged simply but harshly. If its lessons enable you to recoup the cover price it will have been worthwhile. The more business-minded will add that an allowance should also be made for the time spent reading it, at a commercial rate per hour: these folk may make hundreds or even thousands of pounds from *How to Make Money from Antiques*, and this is as it should be.

Helpful, straightforward advice has been my aim — especially in the section on auctions, an arena that often intimidates the tyro. Ignorance is never bliss in the saleroom, and auctioneers and their assistants much prefer dealing with clients who know the drill, talk the same language (or jargon) and who save them time and trouble. The machinations of the dreaded 'ring' (see Chapter 4) are also covered, but most of us, in truth, have more to fear from Wagner's Ring than the saleroom's. All a seller need do to thwart the ring is to set a sensible reserve price, below which his goods cannot be sold.

This is probably the first book that recognises the fact that the antiques world is inhabited by people as well as things — and that sometimes the people are more interesting. Anyone considering entering a new occupation should always look at the people already in it. Antique dealers often look fraught, overworked and harassed; when you read this book you will understand why. The winners, however, look like successful people in every other profession: well groomed, poised, smartly dressed, and with the elegance of the truly solvent. A complete chapter devoted to these paragons has been included.

Anyone can join the antiques club, regardless of age, sex, education or background. Commercial flair cannot be taught, but techniques can be copied and adapted; and there are other ways in which to score points (and earn cash), through greater experience or deeper understanding of a subject.

In fact, there are more ways to make money from antiques than is generally realised. You can sell them, auction them, write about them (many dealers do, and gain in stature from having their names on an erudite volume); antiques can be shipped (Michael Davis, shipper, won a Queen's Award for Export and Achievement for his efforts in this direction — see Chapter 6); antiques can be hired for gain, and they can even earn money doing nothing — as the museum men (see Chapter 5) have discovered to their advantage. It is even possible to profit from providing an environment in which others can trade in antiques. The best known entrepreneur in this mould must be Bennie Gray (see Chapter 6).

At whichever point you want to come into the market, it is no use dreaming about it. You have to start, and the sooner the better. This book, dedicated to the dabbler, has been written to help you get started quickly and painlessly. With energy and luck it could turn you into a professional.

MEL LEWIS
London, May 1980

[1]

The Antique Trade

Until the 1960s, antique dealers enjoyed a variety of popular images. Whether male or female, they were easily recognised stereotypes and carried with them an image of the trade which was more fanciful than accurate. Such stereotypes would themselves be museum pieces today — never mind their stock in trade. Today's antique specialist (full-time trader, part-timer or collector/dealer) can be anyone with the time, energy, dedication, flair and sheer business sense enough to make the grade.

I once was told by a London cab driver that becoming a taxi driver was the last stand of the independent man. The story quickly emerged of businesses that had failed and dreams that had faded. A lot of people came into antiques similarly by the back door. Dealing in antiques was a favourite sideline of resting actresses; rag and bone merchants who discovered that one person's junk was another's gem became antique dealers; interior decorator types were drawn in by the prettiness of some antiques. Many who drifted in have by now drifted out; for the lessons that needed to be learned were hard ones. Today more than ever before antiques is a business, booming at the top — the famous London saleroom of Sotheby's recorded a net sales total of £ 94,335,000 for 1979, more than 31 per cent up on their previous year's results — and it is very hard work at many other levels.

There are stories of stocks drying up; of the exodus of the American as a powerful buying force, with the hardening of the dollar against other international currencies; of the rise of the Italian, French, Dutch and German dealers who buy up stock on sight, leaving little for the small man to play with. In the six months running up to the beginning of 1980, prominent British pine specialists found themselves going to the wall. Their businesses had been geared to shipping container-loads of pine, where it was a matter of 'never mind the quality, feel the width'. The mainstay of their erstwhile successful businesses was the 'cod' (trade jargon for 'chest of drawers'). Dealers who were sending perhaps fifty cods to the Continent, and taking little over £4 profit on each of them, soon found themselves in difficulties. The margin for retail trade at home had advanced enormously; but the rate the shipper was getting for his cods had not improved nearly as much — partly because a chest often needs considerable work doing to it. Supply, however, was the big problem. As suppliers saw the greater cash potential at home, they were reluctant to sell out (even wholesale) to 'cheap-skate' shipping merchants.

Collectors who became professionals

Nevertheless, for every story of someone who fails, there are two of those who have succeeded. Some of the most fascinating tales are those about collectors who became dealers.

Dealing in Oriental art is a daunting prospect to many. Yet now that quality antique Orientalia can be bought cheaper in London than in, say, Hong Kong, and Japanese dealers are finding it worth their while to travel half-way across the world to buy in the UK, it is well worth discovering how you might begin. While he was working in public relations, George Horan began to build up a collection of Oriental objects, and what started out as a hobby turned into a way of life. The collection grew and Mr. Horan, who had come to the UK from Australia in 1939, married a British girl; both grew fascinated with their chosen subject. They read extensively, bought continuously until, one day, they looked around and discovered that their home had been taken over by the collection. It was then that they decided to deal, only in a small way at first; then they took premises over an antique shop in London's Bond Street, and began to sell from their own collection. Today they operate from London's Kensington Church Street and have a wide following of dealers, who, they insist, are more like friends than customers.

George Horan likes to inform others about his subject; he lectures on Orientalia, Chinese art in particular, to collectors' clubs and adult education centres. The sign on the door says 'Come in and browse' — and it is meant. The Horans go out of their way to make their customers feel at home: 'We have a never-ending tea ceremony in the shop. Clients come in for a cup of tea and a chat — and we create a friendly atmosphere.'

The window of Oriental Antiques bears a CD plate. This means that their antiques have been vetted and approved by the *Corps Diplomatique*. Oriental Antiques is one of the few premises to have earned this cachet, which is a most lucrative source of business. Today, items from the Horans' shop adorn embassies throughout the world.

Former bank manager Mr Onslow-Cole, a lifelong hobbyist, managed to turn his interest in clocks into a thriving business. He was offered early retirement, set up a shop, and has never looked back. Today, Onslow Clocks has one of the largest collections of longcase clocks in the London area. They also have quality bracket clocks, French, dial, and wall clocks, and deal mostly with the private collector. Mr Onslow-Cole was not drawn into dealing blindly: from his premises in Twickenham, Middlesex, he said that clock prices have risen by 30 per cent in a year: 'Clocks have long been undervalued. They are superb examples of craftsmanship — especially when you consider that the makers had to fashion their own tools.' Another strong pointer for an increasing value accruing to clocks and watches is the fact that traditional mechanisms are fast disappearing, along with their associated skills, as the quartz revolution takes over.

The Singing Tree Dolls' House shop, in London's New King's Road, is yet another example of a collector-to-dealer story come true with resounding success. Ann Griffith and Thalia Saunders both collected dolls' houses, and their friends made pretty accessories for their collections. After much coaxing, the friends were persuaded to make these dolls' house items a paying proposition. Now the shop features the work of over eighty British craftsmen, much of it exclusive to the Singing Tree. Not only have Ann and Thalia prospered, but the craftsmen who supply their goods have, in some cases, been able to devote themselves full-time to their miniature master-pieces.

One of the best known collectors turned dealers is Bryan Catley. He is co-owner of Catspa Antiques in the Georgian village, Camden Passage, London. He specialises in art deco and art nouveau figures in bronze, ivory and marble. He was left a figure by his grandmother and liked it, and as a student began buying figures for his own pleasure. At Maples twelve years ago he bought a figure by Preiss called 'Con Brio'. It cost £12, and being in mint condition is today worth perhaps £1,800. Catley was lucky enough to amass a fine collection, which has formed the backbone of his business, and all of it was acquired at rock-bottom prices. Since then, of course, he has added to his collection from all the normal sources; but few can match the vast knowledge and experience he has gained over the years.

Philip Walker and Roy Arnold were running their business, selling mainly woodworking tools, from a large house in Balham, south London, when I first met them. Then, as business grew, and their beautifully produced catalogue, *The Traditional Tools of the Carpenter and Other Craftsmen,* became known and their reputation gained in stature, they were obliged to move out of London to more suitable premises, at Needham Market in Suffolk. They had met through their interest in amateur cabinet-making and in 1974 decided to turn that hobby into a commercial operation. Their stock rapidly became the most comprehensive collection of tools in Britain. Then, in 1979, they decided to end their association and auction their entire stock — some 6,000 items. Their brief but profitable partnership had also yielded, in the catalogues, a unique historic record for the future. When the tools came under the hammer on 23 and 24 April 1979, at Christie's South Kensington, the two men were handsomely rewarded for their time and scholarship when the entire takings for the sale came to £62,789.

Dealing from home

Many dealers find it convenient and economical to trade from home. It means they are often available after hours to busy travelling traders or Continental buyers, and also they do not have to pay two sets of rates, rent or twice the mortgage. Desmond and Amanda North trade from their Georgian house on the outskirts of East Peckham, near Tonbridge in Kent. They also have substantial grounds around the house, so twice a year they hold a 'rug-in'. Over a weekend, usually at the end of May and at the beginning of October, they spread out their entire stock of oriental rugs, carpets and runners on the surrounding lawns and yew hedges. If the weather is not fine, they display their wares under canvas, in two large marquees.

The attraction of antiques

Even people who are not collectors are keen to get into antiques. I know an accounts controller on a national newspaper who left a secure position to help run an antique shop. A relative of mine, once in the clothes trade, now deals in silver and Sheffield plate. A secretary I once hired now runs a stall part-time in a local antique market. Frustrated history buffs, craftsmen and artists abound. Working with beautiful, often handmade items is pure pleasure to many in this machine age. In certain areas, notably porcelain, the most 'bookish' of the specialities, the ability to research and retain information is vital; and in any area of antiques the more you know the better equipped are you to succeed (see Chapter 3). Hard work pays dividends in antiques, the old fashioned justness of which appeals to some.

Antiques bring out the hunting instinct in both men and women. Tales of treasures found and lost act as bait to the unwary, the auction houses being particularly adept at weaving sensational finds into their publicity material — like the plate which for years had served as a flower pot stand and turned out to be late fourteenth century blue and white Ming. It made £18,000 in 1979 at Sotheby's. The curious owner of a carved piece of wood took it to Sotheby's and learned that it was a Carolingian ivory depicting St. John the Evangelist. Dating to the early ninth century, the ivory came under the hammer for £225,000 in December, 1977. There was also the coal shed curio that a man sold to a leading London dealer for £650. It turned out to be an ancient Egyptian sandstone figurine and the dealer sold it to a Berlin museum for £26,900. A blackened cast iron fire fender sold for a fortune when it was discovered that it had merely been painted black as a token of respect when Queen Victoria died. Underneath the paint was not iron but solid silver.

Such stories are meat and drink to the amateur; the professional merely shrugs his shoulders and gets on with the business of turning over goods for the profit he knows he can reasonably take. When he is out of pocket, that too is part of the daily round — he only hopes that he will not be in such difficulty that he will have to let his find go for less than the best he could obtain.

The business of antiques

To make money in antiques you do not normally need to be a connoisseur. A 'feel for the market' (buying the right thing at the right price) comes with knowledge and experience. Reading helps; talking to experts is even better; handling top quality is vital. In the end, however, the essential is a 'money mentality': the ability to do deals. To prove the point, the antique markets have spawned a type of operator who appears to have no special commitment to antiques. He or she merely flits from stall to stall noting the prices of similar objects. Sometimes it is not even necessary to take the chance of speculative buying. For so finely tuned is the mind of such marketeers that they are able to describe their finds to traders in another part of the market and be commissioned on the spot. Profit may be only a pound or two on each deal, but an energetic morning's work can yield a fair day's pay.

A businessman uncle of mine who had just retired with 'more money than I need for the rest of my days' once said, 'What is business, but the ability to buy something for a pound and sell it for two?' He was right, of course; but the statement, when applied to antiques, begs many questions. What should you buy, where and how? What is the right price to pay? How and where do you sell, and to whom? The answers, or at least a determined attempt at them, form the nub of this book. Some questions, such as 'What is the right amount of mark-up?' have no exact answers. So much intimate information is lacking, such as the individual's overheads, how long he can afford to wait to take a profit, and the expenses involved in selling. Selling at a major London auction room has become extremely expensive, as this quotation from The Economist Intelligence Unit Ltd's 1980 publication *Art as Investment* shows (*pro rata* for lesser amounts):

'On an item with a selling price of £100,000 these charges, net of transport, can be assessed as:

	£
Hammer Price	100,000
Insurance premium	500
Vendor's commission	10,000
VAT at 15 per cent	1,500
Net return to vendor	88,000

Thus, without taking any account of transport costs and packing, a vendor resident in the UK who sells through a major auctioneer can expect to receive 88 per cent of the hammer price. If the item the vendor is offering for sale is illustrated in the sale catalogue a further charge is normally made, on which VAT is payable.'

A question of acute importance to the dealer selling to the dealer is: 'At what price will the person I am selling to be able to take a profit that he considers adequate?' 'There's nothing in it for me,' the buyer complains when the price is not right. Susan Becker opened her Putney antique shop in the early 1960s. Occasionally she bought for £50 and sold for £200. More often the mark-up was 15 to 20 per cent — and she was putting in sixteen hours' work from 7 am in the early days. Some dealers aim at 100 per cent mark-up when selling to the trade. When the customer is a private person, 300 per cent is not unusual. Generally, the more expensive the goods, the smaller the margin of profit; top quality paintings can change hands for only a 15 or 10 per cent improvement.

The need to assess status and profit 'needs' also helps to explain why antiques are so often unpriced or marked with a price code. If a dealer wants you to break his code he may use the simplest one: A = 1, B = 2, C = 3, and so on. Alternatively, he might start further down the alphabet, just to confuse. Sometimes the trade is told how much it can have off: 'T1 or T½; — 1 or — ½' means less £1 or 50p. The coding also protects the shopkeeper from the private buyer who goes in for comparison shopping. The private buyer who asks 'What is your best trade price?' can inadvertently come unstuck. For buying at trade or wholesale price can exclude him from the cover provided by the consumer protection laws. It subjects him to the principle *caveat emptor* (let the buyer beware): once the purchaser has made his purchase he is expected to stand by his judgement. Furthermore, the dealer is at liberty to ask for credentials as proof of professional status. In reality, this rarely happens; dealers just seem to know whether you are in or outside the trade, and treat you accordingly.

The antiques marketplace is attractive because it is eccentric. Almost everything is unique, even identical items being differentiated by their condition. There is no recommended retail price: the selling and the buying price is created in a particular economic climate. Bennie Gray, owner of London's leading antique markets, says that when he was young (he is now only in his forties) he was able to buy Burne-Jones drawings for £5; now they are museum pieces. Impressionist paintings, were, by current values, grossly underpriced prior to about 1958 and that legendary Sotheby's auction at which seven pictures made £781,000. 'Intrinsic artistic worth' of an item is a matter for conjecture; it will not get you a bank loan; but a written valuation from a reputable auctioneer might. Everything has a value. Who would have thought even a few years ago that a collection of Victorian woodworking tools could have fetched the price of a big house at auction; that there would be collectors of Bakelite radios, Dinky toys and Mickey Mouse memorabilia; that Edwardian Sheraton-style furniture and honeyed oak Tudor-style furniture from the 1930s would have a following; that a market would develop for fake pictures? How many times has it been said that you should buy only what antiques you like? The dictum 'buy only what you like' is fine for the collector, but not much use to the trader. A corollary goes 'buy what you like and someone else will like it, too'. Today you can be sure that whether you like it or not *someone* will have it.

The power of cash

One of the problems of our fiscal civilization has been the abandonment of real money. We have long since forgotten what gold and silver coin was like to handle, and now the trend is firmly in favour of cheques and credit cards. Nevertheless, this has not diminished the power of cash in the form of bank notes; it has enhanced it. Most antique trade buying and selling at any but the highest levels is, let it be said, on a cash basis. So also is that between a private customer and a trader, though most accept cheques and some will take credit cards. If you understand the fascination of banknotes you can turn even minor purchases into major victories — and learn a little of the dealing arts into the bargain.

I first came across the 'money lust' some years ago. I was interested in collectable motor cars at that time, and happened to notice a 'frogeye' Sprite (Austin-Healey) that I liked the look of in a nearby street. A note through the window indicating that I was interested in buying did the trick: the owner telephoned and we discussed a possible price and arranged to meet. He wanted £260. I had about £250, but, not wanting to starve for the rest of the week, I made a bundle of 230 pound notes and stuffed them into a back pocket.

At the appropriate moment (the owner had half-heartedly suggested dropping to £250) I declared that £230 was all I had, but he could have the lot there and then. We were sitting on opposite sides of a table, and I put the bank roll, which opened like a flower, in front of him, within reach. The car owner said not another word but reached for the money and the deal was complete.

For example, at an antique stall in a British market you might operate like this. Carry several wads of notes of different denominations in different pockets and a few single £1 and £5 notes and 50p pieces in another pocket or bag. (You must remember where everything is; it is no use to say that you only have another pound and then bring out a fiver!) See which items you want. Suppose there is a piece of crested china for £6.50, a brass pot for £3 and a teapot for £10. If you bought the china separately you might get 50p off or at best £1. If you bought just the brass pot 50p off might be top whack. Together, at the marked prices, you must pay £9.50. So you offer £7, thinking that the stallholder will resist this and suggest £8. He does. You give him a fiver — in his hand — and hesitate. You produce two more fivers. 'How about this teapot for £15 the lot?' The dealer had expected to receive only another three pound notes and here he is on the receiving end of three fivers. Likely as not he will agree — and you have your teapot for £7, a phenomenal saving of 30 per cent, which would have been out of the question if you had purchased the teapot alone.

Once you know how to prune prices, you can work out more complex accumulating deals on the spot and end up with substantial savings. Occasionally a dealer will get upset. He will refuse to come down, or, if you push too hard, will refuse to trade with you. The answer to this is to move on, and get a friend to buy whatever it was you wanted on the first stall.

Keeping a constant look-out for trade

The enterprising dealer or would-be dealer is always looking for trade and the means of turning over a profit. On holiday in Cornwall recently I discovered an establishment worthy of the title curio shop, one of the few. It was an Aladdin's cave of low price items that must yield a small profit in London. For £6.50

there was 'a pair of legs' — two massive mahogany limbs, with
carved knee and scroll foot, that had come from some giant
mid-Victorian washstand or hall table. They were ostensibly
useless, but there is a wine bar in Camden Passage in which an
odd cabriole leg is used to add interest to a boring corner of the
ceiling. The decorator trade would love them, and pay perhaps
£12 the pair. There were four framed bronze wall plaques
depicting the MPs Balfour, Chamberlain, Lloyd George and
Asquith. The backs showed unmistakable signs of natural
ageing; the lettering was typical of the Edwardian era. I
concluded that they were contemporary. Given the fine
moulding of the portraits, dating from history books would be
easy. They appeared to be unsigned. They may turn out to be
by a famous artist and so more important than I thought. I
doubted, however, if they would be less important. I guessed
that they would sell for a fairly easy £35 the four or £10 each,
at a minimum. They were priced at £17.50 the set. I offered £15
and settled at £16.

The shop had other things, too, all of which could in my
estimation have been turned over for profit. There was an
unusual trivet, for example, at £4.50, for propping a hot iron at
an angle. That could be used as a plate rest, for display, and
would make £8.50 in London. A simple Victorian wooden peg
box about 2 ft 6 in by 2 ft (76 x 61 cm) was £9.50. Without
tumbling houseplants in it, its charms were unrealised.
Properly displayed it would fetch £15. There were two brush and
pan sets, one scalloped like a shell, the other deeply engraved,
both brass. One set was £7.50, the other £6.50. Why the
difference? The cheaper had a near bald brush, and was spoiled
because of it. Nevertheless the other would fetch £10 in London.

This is the sort of buying the low-level trader needs to do
week in week out, and of course the more that is paid the more
can be chipped off the marked price of individual items as well
as the total price. What about the cost of travelling and
accommodation, however? What about the better profit a
dealer might have picked up if he had been in his shop when a
certain customer called rather than out on the road? A dealer,
now one of the most successful in Islington, explains how, when
he first set up shop, he stocked up with the personal antiques
that had decorated his own home. In the first week he took £200
profit. He was over the moon. That profit, however, was based
on the little he had paid for the items long ago. Restocking at

current prices swallowed most of his takings; nor was finding suitable stock an easy matter. Finding stock is one of the professional's biggest headaches, and explains why so often you see reproduction furniture, brass and copper, sitting uneasily alongside the few bits of genuine antiques the dealer has been able to muster. I have heard it said that the test of a true dealer comes when he buys something and is unable to sell it because he has fallen in love with it. I fear that we are heading into an era in which the true dealer is one who stays in business; who having fallen in love with something is nevertheless able to sell it — though he may boost the price sufficiently to sugar his disappointment.

[2]
Choosing
an Area of Antiques

What type of antiques should you choose to trade in? There are many factors to consider, some obvious, others less so. If you are frail, for example, you would not consider bulky, heavy furniture; if you plan on running a small stall, longcase clocks are not recommended; and so on. A collector can use his collection as stock, as frequently happens, although shifts of interest are quite common, and it is not unknown for a specialist of long standing to sell out completely, possibly at auction, and then start up again as a specialist in a totally different area. Nevertheless, most beginners start in a small way, with a small amount of stock, and, more often than not, with 'smalls' — porcelain, glass, jewellery, bric-à-brac, indeed anything easily portable, including small furniture.

Without a ready-made stock, or an over-riding interest to guide you, there are some general points that can be valuable when it comes to choosing a direction; and remember that specialist dealers who never veer from a narrow path are few and far between. Even a picture dealer needs a table to stand a pot of flowers on, and weary customers need chairs, so why not sell those, too? A dealer's furniture needs brightening up; a dresser decked with plates makes a good display, and opens up the opportunity for a porcelain sideline. Besides, strict specialisation is difficult; stock may be hard to find and trade can be slow in coming round — although a lot of money can change hands when the ship does come in. Buyers beat a path to the door of a man who has cornered the market in a particular field, but it is often tempting (and rewarding) for the specialist dealer to spread his net a little.

There is a dealer in antique smoothing irons who keeps ivory figurines and small pieces of oak as a subsidiary interest. The only connection is the prettiness of the pieces. He finds that his

14

customers appreciate a little variety. As many buyers are from overseas, small items nestle nicely in the same pack and cost little extra to transport. A King's Road dealer in planters and *jardinières* has a certain amount of garden statuary as well; his clients are often decorators thinking of their patios or gardens and the association, in their eyes, is an attractive one.

A further argument in favour of diluting a main interest is that the energetic antique dealer is out and about so much he is bound to come across good buys that it would be foolish to turn down. This, of course, is how the general dealer is born and operates, and increasingly specialist dealers are having to break out of the straitjacket of their chosen field in order to turn over enough money to live and grow.

There is a type of lateral thinking that can be useful to the tyro who is unsure where to begin. A classic rule of business is that where one person has a virtual monopoly there is almost always room for a close rival also to make a healthy profit. Antiques that are usable will always have a following. As the price of new furniture rises, so antiques look increasingly attractive buys — even to those who have no declared taste for the old. Musical instruments, notably wind instruments, violins, guitars and banjos, are bought, sometimes in preference to new. There is also a tiny section of antiques that are virtually indispensable to the dealer. Almost every dealer needs a display case, and the modern versions look hideously out of place. There must be a market a-begging for the specialist who deals in nothing but *empty* display cases. Rare small antiques, such as watches, snuff boxes or netsuke, are in constant demand. The thinking seems to be that in times of trouble it would always be possible to pocket the lot and run!

Collectables with a wide catchment area of interest must be strong contenders for the future. A lot of people are keen on photography and many are becoming interested in the history of their subject. Even quite recent cameras, like the twin-lens Rolleiflex and early Leicas, are now worth quite large amounts of money. Fishing is said to be the most popular sport in the UK: one dealer trades in almost nothing but books on fishing. Sporting antiques generally are a neglected area. Nevertheless, it is not every dealer who is able to specialise. Many things can prevent this, such as lack of knowledge, money or opportunity to buy. Some have made their names (and their fortunes) from buying the type of antique that other dealers do not want. The forte of The Old Bellows in Disley, Cheshire, is spectacular

A collector's cabinet. Almost every dealer and collector needs display cabinets. Consequently, there is surely a potential market for a dealer specialising in nothing but empty display cabinets.

antiques (otherwise known as decorator items). Typical stock includes blackamoor figures, large bronzes and globes, large porcelain Minton storks, oversize *jardinières*, king-size bronzes, and so on. They also specialise in longcase clocks and are keen on Continental timepieces with unusual mechanisms, including those that strike on tubes or play bells. Spectacular or grotesque antiques are not everybody's taste; not everyone has room, either. The Old Bellows, however, begun only a few years ago, has found a market — its hinterland includes the homes of prosperous stockbrokers who are well able to afford the £200 to £10,000 price range. Even if private individuals cannot afford oversize items, there is always a call for such antiques from theatrical and film companies. The aim, says their Mr David Dickenson, is to become the most 'fantastic display' outside London.

'Difficult' antiques are worth investigating, if you have the right turn of mind. People are often frightened by gadgetry and figures, dealers being no exception. Anyone who is not can quickly acquaint himself with a tricky topic and capitalise on his expertise.

When Molly Freeman was divorced and left with two young children, there was nothing for it: she had to go to work. She tried selling popcorn and working in an electronics factory but that was not much fun. She was drawn into working with beautiful things and spent some time in porcelain. She even managed to write a book on the subject before giving it up. Then, as she says, 'one day I bought two sextants and I was in business.' Harriet Wynter (the *nom de bataille* of Mrs Freeman) now runs a specialist collectors' shop. She deals in scientific instruments, navigational aids, microscopes, and other items in related fields.

She claims that anybody can successfully collect anything if they constantly read, and forever look and examine: 'This is how you educate yourself and evolve your own taste.' Every time she discovered an unusual instrument, she learned something more about it; she read relevant books on physics and navigation in order to understand more about her esoteric subject; she even went to navigation school. Eventually, together with Anthony Turner, she wrote a well-respected book for collectors on her subject. As a final accolade, she was the first dealer to show scientific instruments at the prestigious Grosvenor House Antiques Fair. She has even ventured into publishing: *Geomagnetic Instruments Before 1900*, by Anita

McConnel, was recently published by Mrs Freeman, alias Mrs Wynter.

A radio ham could make profitable use of the fact that valve radios are now all but obsolete, but the rich melodious sound is enjoying a vogue, and the handsomely fretted or moulded cases of the early receivers are already an established collectable on the antiques scene. It seems inevitable that with the quartz revolution even quite ordinary clocks and watches with traditional movements are likely to gain vastly in price as their status grows and the skills to keep them going become a lost art.

It is essential not to consider stock as collectables. Of course you should be interested in what you sell, but far more important is a readiness of supply and the fair certainty that you can turn over a profit. The stall of William Norton, a Londoner, always attracted a lot of attention at antique fairs, for ever since his father, an oculist, had given him a few fake eyes to use as marbles, William had been a collector of artificial eyes. Although everyone stared at his glassy stock, few actually bought anything...

The following are key areas of current interest and, in my opinion, worthy of closer inspection.

Photographic images

What was it about old photographs that enabled collectors to shun them for years? Was it the apparently facile nature of the medium; the fact that almost everyone owns a camera; that anyone who knows how to press a doorbell can take a picture? One is reminded of the apocryphal story told by Henry Geldzahler, a curator of contemporary painting at the Metropolitan Museum, New York, who, while at Yale, was so irked by an endless debate on whether photography was a science or an art, raised his hand and said he had always thought it was a hobby.

There may have been other factors at work, stifling interest in such easily available Victoriana as photographs once were. One such factor may have been the ease with which photographs are reproduced from negatives, quite overlooking the fact that the old negatives or plates had almost certainly been lost or had perished, and that some of the most stunning early images, the daguerreotypes, had no negative at all. Each daguerreotype was unique, a limited edition of one; built-in rarity that should have had the collectors and dealers scurrying. Curiously, however, it did not, until the 1970s. There was also the fact that the camera, far from never lying, is frequently made to tell fibs. There was an uneasy suspicion that fakes, being easily executed, must have been often made. Why waste time and money faking an image if it could not be sold for a swift cash profit? No market must have meant no 'murk' — which is not to say that there is no forgery today. There surely is, but only in the higher echelons of the game, which will not concern the average reader.

Attempting to sum up the appeal of photography and its future potential for the collector, Alan Shestack, in a foreword to *The Photograph Collector's Guide* (Secker & Warburg), writes: '...the widespread interest in photography...means that there is an enormous audience for serious photography. People

An Antarctic landscape from a collection of approximately 70 contact photographs of Scott's 1910-13 expedition. Sold in a group for £260. [Courtesy of Christie's South Kensington.]

who have tried their hand at picture-making can understand the visual and technical problems that confront the photographer trying to capture a particular mood or image and can thus begin to perceive the differences between amateur photographs and professional ones, between clichés and creative statements.' The author of the book, Lee D. Witkin, a keen collector and gallery owner, continues in a more commercial vein: 'The opportunity to collect well without investing large amounts of money is present today in photography as in none of the other arts.' Mr Witkin is talking about present-day as well as vintage photographs. It is helpful here to glance, briefly, backwards at the history of photography.

The story of photography begins with a retired French army officer, Joseph Nicéphore Niepce, who in 1827 produced the first successful photograph. His 'film' was pewter plates coated with bitumen, developed in a solution of lavender oil and white petroleum. His historic first picture from life, of rooftops and a barn taken through his window, is badly blurred; it took eight hours of exposure to achieve. Later, Niepce teamed up with Louis Daguerre who was able to cut exposure time down to an hour. Daguerre used silver-plated copper plate coated with light sensitised silver iodide. By 1841 a daguerreotype could be produced in 20 seconds, and, not long after, fast enough for portraiture. Photography caught on like wildfire, studios opening up all over the world to cater for the new craze. Nevertheless, the daguerreotype suffered from a serious drawback: the image could not easily be reproduced. So the vast market for repeat orders, copy prints, could not be tapped.

As early as 1834 William Henry Fox Talbot, a British aristocrat, had produced photographic prints on paper which he washed in a salt solution. Astronomer Sir John Herschel (later to be immortalised in photographic portraits by Julia Margaret Cameron) co-operated with Fox Talbot and the result was the calotype or talbotype — a salted paper print taken from a paper negative. The calotype was the first negative/positive photograph and prints could be taken from it in quantity. Frederick Scott Archer invented the wet-plate process in 1851; the film was actually wet while it was in the camera. Though messy in use, the resulting image was sharp and exposure time was short. At first the more convenient dry-plate process was slower and all sorts of treatments were tried, to speed up exposure time. Extract of sherry, beer, tea, treacle, honey and vinegar were all used. No wonder the photographic experiments of the mid nineteenth century have become known as the 'culinary period'! The first paper-backed roll film, heralding the modern era in photography, was produced by Kodak in 1888.

Daguerreotypes are relatively easy to recognise. There is a metallic sheen to the surface. Turned one way the image is pin sharp; turned slightly away the picture disappears in a silvery haze. Daguerreotypes were often framed in jewellery; gold and pinchbeck mounts are known. Similarly framed were the ambrotypes, images printed on glass and produced in the 1850s – 60s as a cheap alternative. The ferrotype or tintype, patented in 1856, cheaper still, used lacquered sheet iron. A grey look can denote an ambrotype, while ferrotypes have a blackish look and metallic sheen.

The daguerreotype, ambrotype and ferrotype were all one-off photographs and similarly framed and mounted, edged in pinchbeck, encased in leather, velvet, papier mâché or leatherette. An American patent of 1854 was for a gum, shellac and wood fibre case, sometimes press moulded into exotic relief patterns, rather in the style of repoussé silver. Calotypes are recognisable with experience. The print has a rough surface, rather like laid writing paper. A good pointer is if the paper carries the papermaker's watermark: Turner, of Chalfont Mills, was a noted supplier.

It is essential to be able to spot the various types of photographs and there is much helpful literature around. The section entitled 'A Collector's Glossary' in the earlier-mentioned *The Photograph Collector's Guide* advises: 'The best way to become familiar with different media is to learn the facts, then examine and compare specimens.' The glossary gives the facts, as does an appendix to Helmut and Alison Gernsheim's *Masterpieces of Victorian Photography* (Phaidon). A useful primer is *Victorian Photography, A Collector's Guide*, by B.E.C. Howarth-Loomes (Ward Lock), and the Gernsheims' *magnum opus, The History of Photography* (Thames and Hudson), is the definitive work for photographica enthusiasts.

The facts about the lineage of photography (only briefly touched upon here) are available to everybody. The ability to evolve a strategy for acquiring images is another matter, as is the ability to implement it successfully and ultimately to turn over a profit. There is much written about finding treasure in the attic, and certainly people have discovered dust-covered albums which yielded undreamed-of treasures when placed under the hammer. The chance of coming up trumps, of discovering, in a sepia-tinged print, that a long-forgotten ancestor once hobnobbed with the famous, exists. Nevertheless, you will get nowhere in the antique world if you propose to rely on such 'long shots'.

In photography, the saleroom is the crucible of the market, and, in the UK, the front runners are Christie's South Kensington and Sotheby's Belgravia. A sixth-plate or quarter-plate daguerreotype, in a folding morocco case, portrait of an unidentified sitter by an unnamed photographer, should cost £20–25. Named daguerreotypists enhance value; notable exponents were Antoine François Jean Claudet and Richard Beard. Claudet carried the torch from Louis Jacques Mandé Daguerre, the inventor himself, from France to London, where he opened a studio in 1841, shortly after Beard had similarly set up shop. Claudet is renowned for hand-coloured daguerreotypes featuring elaborate backdrops. In 1853 he became official

HMS Dauntless at anchor, one of two fine sixth-plate daguerreotype studies of the stern and broadside, 1853. Sold for £500. [Courtesy of Christie's South Kensington.]

photographer to Queen Victoria. Beard is also famous for his hand-colouring.

Intriguing and stirring glimpses of history, thrilling to all and sundry, are reflected in the £650 paid at Christie's South Kensington in 1980 for each of two views of sailing ships. A more idiosyncratic taste noticed that a lady in a daguerreotype portrait for sale at Sotheby's Belgravia had an artificial hand, and the price for this oddity escalated to £620 (one collector buys daguerreotypes showing people with eye deformities). Bizarre images, like the small boy with a vast pompadour of a hairstyle, also make over-the-odds prices, as do morbid scenes of dead children. Ordinary domestic photographs which feature an early household or kitchen gadget (or a maid) are also popular. A scientific instrument used in the background or as a prop will boost value.

In the pioneering days, photography was a rich man's pastime, so working class scenes are desirable and pricey. Stereoscopic daguerreotypes are also known but you will need a stereoscopic viewer (a Victorian one, of course) to appreciate fully the three-dimensional effect. Among the most sought-after daguerreotypes are nudes. Nude studies are hotly pursued in all period photographic media, as was evidenced at the October 1978 sale at Christie's South Kensington, when the only recorded nude study by Roger Fenton (famed for his Crimean War photographs) was sold for £3,600.

The Victorians threw themselves into their hobby with customary energy and application — even Queen Victoria and her beloved Albert had their own darkroom. The 1851 Exhibition featured work by many leading practitioners, including Robert Adamson and David Hill, the artist; ironically you would now pay more for one of Hill's photographs than for one of his painted portraits. Other names to note are Francis Frith, Felice A. Beato (who, together with James Robertson, photographed 'aftermaths' of the Crimean War: the intricate wet-plate process they used making action photography impossible), and the pioneers of 'artistic' photography — O. G. Rejlander and Henry Peach Robinson. In 1857 Rejlander's composite work, *Two Ways of Life*, caused a sensation among the photographic *cognoscenti* in England, and Robinson also began combining negatives to create romantic idylls of country life, depicting peasants and lush countryside. One print showed a dying girl surrounded by grieving relatives: it had been concocted from five negatives. The romantic genre, which may well set today's teeth on edge, was popular at that time and reflects the early photographers' fierce determination to compete with brush artists and to go beyond mere statements of momentary fact.

The soft focus portraiture of Julia Margaret Cameron is among the finest photographic work ever executed, and this has been amply recognised in the salerooms, where four-figure prices for a single shot are not uncommon. More accessible are old albums full of views of faraway places, such as Australia, Canada or Hong Kong. The early practitioners rarely got that far — or came back safely and with their work intact. Francis Frith, one of the most prolific English photographers, earned a reputation as a travelling photographer in the late 1850s, grappling with the complexities of the collodion wet-plate process at one time 1,500 miles up the Nile. His views of the Sphinx and Great Pyramid caused a sensation and Frith enjoyed considerable success, later opening his own studio in Reigate. Late Frith work may not have been by the master, as it is known that he bought in negatives of other artists merely to print. Nevertheless, it is still worth owning named Frith images.

Carte-de-visite photographs are tipped as a lively area, worthy of further exploration. The original idea was of a pictorial visiting card, a genuine little photograph of the presenter. The most popular size, however, was larger, 2½ in × 4 in. It was the popular equivalent, in the period 1857 to 1862, of the modern Polyfoto. Sitters were encouraged to pose for a session which would produce six to a dozen portraits. (In 1854 André Adolphe Eugène Disdéri had patented the idea of a camera which could take a series of likenesses on one plate with a single exposure.) The *carte-de-visite* was not only fun for all the Victorian family, but it also became a status game and a great fad, with diminutive snapshots of criminals, Siamese twins, the Royal canines, animals and politicians, all eagerly collected. By the close of the century a larger size image, about 4 in × 6 in, the cabinet portrait, caught on, and it is the unfamiliar glimpse of a famous face that is most prized today.

Albums of old photographs are often found as one lot in the saleroom, or hidden under a pile of old sheet music in a junk shop. A decrepit binding and damp spotting on the pages inside are no cause for alarm. What does matter is the condition of the pictures. It is advisable to shun marked images, since renovation is tricky and expensive.

Old pine

Familiarity usually breeds contempt, but not in the case of pine. The more we see it, apparently, the more we love it. No antiques thoroughfare is complete without a stripped pine shop; the furniture chainstores are churning out charmless reproductions in 'green' pine; and many people have enjoyed stripping a paint-caked wheel-back chair or chest of drawers, to reveal the light, fresh bare wood beneath.

The demand for old pine may be inexhaustible, but the supply is not. Pine is still in the low price bracket. Dealers work to a small mark-up, high turnover; one dealer is selling chests to a Frenchman for £30 each. The man takes twenty to forty at a time, minimally stripped; then, with the handles removed, they are packed tight and shipped home. It is not worth his while to pay more. The British dealer is barely reimbursed for his trouble; but given the quantity, and the regular order, it turns into a paying proposition. Before long, his sources could become exhausted.

It seems possible that pine could go the way of 'brown' furniture. The fine, virtually unretouched pieces would then command prices on a par with today's oak and mahogany; experts will be writing monographs on period pine, and the knowledgeable investor/collector will vie with the 'ritzy' dealers at the auction rooms.

That, however, is in a dismal, pessimistic future. Nevertheless, the trading-up trend is beginning to be revealed. Fine pieces of early, unstripped pine (the mid-eighteenth century is the earliest date normally found) are already finding a *recherché* market, but not in Britain. The British will not yet pay the premium on the best unrestored pine, dealers say. So it sells to wealthy East Coast (Pennsylvania, New England) Americans.

Pine, being a softwood, and at the mercy of rot and worm, was also often painted, stained or varnished and this coloured look is an acquired taste. The Swedes, Norwegians and Austrians are avidly hunting their own pine from the period 1750 to 1800. Artists in those parts of the world were known to paint for esteemed cabinet-makers; authoritatively attributed examples of these artists' work (some used characteristic monograms) have been known to fetch £5,000.

In a lively market, both at home and abroad, with prices yet to reach their zenith, and with discernible trends, it should be possible to make profitable headway, even as a beginner. What we see is the market split in a number of ways. There are dealers trading from smart 'decorator' shops, whose greatest contribution to the ready stripped and finished pine they buy is where they place the potted plant or position the blue and white plate in the dresser rack. Other dealers show their rough, half-finished pieces and offer a bespoke service, in which the customer specifies favourite handles, shade of wood, style of moulding if a replacement is needed, and so on. Such a dealer, whose stock may well stand under a flimsy shelter around the caustic stripping bath in his yard, could supply the first type of dealer. The bespoke dealer is, in turn, supplied by a man who travels around the country buying up pine from what can be termed primary sources. These are the cheapest suppliers — and also the most difficult for the tyro to track down. A suave London pine dealer who was foolish enough to reveal his source of supply in a BBC television programme came to regret this when there was a discernible shift of trade from his own store to the West Country dealer he had named! As another dealer put it: 'You need to visit a lot of pubs, listen to a lot of conversations to find suppliers. And they won't be interested unless you can take regular amounts.'

The places to look for pine are areas of intense population, such as the major Northern towns of England. Areas that were densely populated 100 years ago (even if they are not today) are also good potential sources, because, that dealer claims, there was virtually a production line business in pine furniture established in these areas as long ago as the 1800s. The cabinet-makers passed the pieces into the finishing shop where they were given a lime wash, rather like a thin solution of plaster of Paris or gesso, which would fill the grain and smooth over the knots, before painting.

Oak, burr walnut, herringbone and cross-graining were all cleverly faked by painting, and, at the time, popularly received. It must be remembered that oak was the poor man's wood, a substitute for the wealthy city dweller's mahogany and walnut. Country people and the lower orders in town would make do with pine; but they preferred it to look like more expensive woods, and it was doctored accordingly. A dealer had three such original pieces dating to 1840 – 50 and could not sell them. One went eventually to a decorator with an eye for the exotic: he actually liked the 'tiger' look and the fact that the bare pine was beginning to show through from genuine wear rather than artificial treatment. Finally the dealer lost heart and reluctantly stripped the other two. They sold inside a week.

The pastel colours of the immediate post-Regency period are rather more endearing to today's tastes; pale blues and grey pastel shades, sometimes with panelling painted in, imitating the deeply fielded panels of heavy, expensive oak furniture.

Not all pine was painted as a matter of course. A dealer bought a dresser from an old village school, and having stripped the dresser of its murky brown paint discovered it to date to *c.* 1880. It was clear that the dresser had been left bare and scrubbed clean for years; the softwood had worn prettily away to give a characteristic rippled and raised effect. It had probably been painted no earlier than twenty years previously.

Pine dealing appeals as an archetypal small-scale activity; trade can be comfortably carried on from a back garden or modest outbuilding. Certainly it would be possible to supply a retailer in need of only a couple of fresh, finished pieces a week. With a reliable supply and a guaranteed market for finished goods, it could well be possible quickly to sort out cash flow and keep modestly in profit. Once an operation succeeds, however, the temptation to expand becomes irresistible. It is soon time to employ: one man to buy, another to work on the wood, another to sell the completed work. Then five, ten or twenty pieces need to be turned over in a week to pay the wages and overheads and one is forced to buy not at one-off prices from out-of-the-way suppliers but at the going market price, from a known and easily accessible venue. Auction buying of pine is often too unreliable for the professional; firstly, it is time-consuming, and, worse, there is no way of guaranteeing a successful bid. A dealer sometimes tries to corner a market in an area by bidding over the odds. Rival dealers, forced to bide their valuable time, soon tire, and go where their money is better appreciated. Then, needless to say, the tyrant relaxes his intimidation campaign and proceeds to buy at the normal price.

Pine attracts small-time operators also because the carpentry skills involved are often within the scope of the capable handyman. Nevertheless, the preliminary stripping may not be. The liquid used for stripping is sometimes referred to as acid; in fact it is the opposite. It is one of the most powerful alkalis known, caustic soda; the effects, however, are similar to those caused by acid, and great care must be taken to protect the eyes when such liquid is being used. Too often the amateur makes do with too shallow a bath (one professional dealer uses a bath 5 ft deep, 7 ft across and 10 ft long) or overheats the liquid; he may also steep the furniture overlong, and make elementary mistakes like omitting to remove the drawers. Sometimes you see fine clear crystals forming on porous pine, perhaps inside the drawers or round the back. This indicates too long a soaking in the bath. After immersion, thorough washing must follow. Professionals remove not only the drawers but also the catches and doors. The most they soak for is half an hour; better still, it is said, is to 'dunk' the piece three or four times at five-minute intervals; this is especially recommended with delicate or damaged pieces. The only pine which can be safely soaked for long periods is a door, for example, bearing twenty coats of paint. Be sure, nevertheless, that the paint is deep all over, not just on the side previously exposed to the weather. Washing down is sometimes effected with a brush and a dribbling cold water hose; the professional uses a high pressure hose emitting a jet of water at 1500 pounds per square inch.

Mr G. Blanch, a pine dealer of Benenden in Kent, has enlisted the help of a local inventor who has produced a system of stripping in which a hose directs a caustic solution at high pressure on to the furniture. Not only is it useful for delicate structures, but it is also good where a lot of glueing has been done. Naturally, it is essential to wear protective clothing and a visor. As yet, the method is not commercially available.

A new process is being developed in Germany, in which the furniture need not even be dismantled; it is stacked in a room and a chemical or gas removes the paint in a matter of hours. Although the results are said to be perfect, the system costs many thousands of pounds at present.

Finishing is all-important. After thorough drying, applications of a polish made up of equal parts by weight of turpentine and beeswax is recommended. White spirit can be used as the solvent, but it may crystallise the polish. Turpentine is a natural oil and, though expensive, imparts a handsome sheen to pine. Rubbing down with the wax a couple of times a week, for six or seven weeks, and going over it with wire wool, can work wonders. Burnishing and exposure to the air quickly brings up the grain and the knots and a warm patina develops.

Chez Chalons, one of the leading pine dealers, based in Somerset, issue the following guide to pine treatment.

Preparation

1 Allow adequate time for drying after stripping.
2 Carry out necessary repairs.
3 If wood grain has raised and fluffed during stripping then the following procedure should be carried out, by hand, or using orbital sander: Using a 60 grit for heavy sanding
Using a 80 grit for medium sanding
Using a 120 grit for finishing.
If the piece needs very little sanding then using 00 grade wire wool, form a pad and rub firmly with the grain until smooth to the touch.

Finishing

1 We recommend using Colron light oak stain prior to waxing. Follow instructions on can.
2 For wax finishing using 'Chez Chalons' beeswax formula.
3 Apply liberally in circular motions until wood grain is filled, then finish with the grain as smooth as possible and leave overnight for wax to harden.
4 Using 000 grade wire wool buff gently and continue to unfold the wool as it may clog slightly.
5 Buff with soft duster for final finish.

There is an increasing demand for architectural pine pieces, such as the handsomely moulded interior archway of a grand room, staircases, and the pine half panelling which once rose about as high as the dado rail. The high quality of much country pine can be explained by the fact that it was often made by the resident estate carpenter, usually one of a team. Rarely fully employed by his master, he could make useful money on the side by turning out simple furniture for the locals. The odd pine masterpiece, allegedly produced by a gifted amateur, is a rarity, however; the best pine is cabinet-made quality.

Because of the disturbingly high cost of skilled man-hours, many dealers refuse to get involved with extensive restoration, and will actually turn down tatty but classy pine pieces. As one dealer confided, 'We buy a dresser for £200 and expect to sell it to the trade for £300. But if it needs a new base, backboard, and the drawers are shattered, the mark-up becomes ridiculous.' Pine buyers have been scouting outside the UK for years, finding suitable stocks in France and Scandinavia; but British pine is still considered to be the best. Not only is the quality high, but the variety adds spice to the business, as it is

becoming clear that private customers nurture a boastful pride
in owning characteristically regional pine.

There are many pointers to original provenance, not all of
them reliable. West Country pine, it is said, was often treated
with a red lead undercoat prior to painting; this is revealed,
after stripping, by an attractive red sheen. Scottish pine,
however (from the vast coastal forests), was similarly treated.
Large pieces of pine emanated from large Scottish castles, it is
also claimed; but substantial pine furniture came from the
grand houses of North Wales; at any rate, North Wales pine is
generally larger than that to be found in South Wales.

A characteristic North Wales dresser comes with three
drawers in the base, or a false panel sandwiched between the
outside two cupboard doors. The Welsh favoured a half-glazed
style of dresser; two glazed cupboards would be separated by
open shelving. More often than not, this will rest on a
Pembrokeshire dog kennel style of base (the opening just the
right size to take a great stone jar) flanked by cupboards.
Glazed cupboards were a West Country favourite, though fewer
complete dressers (top, with matching bottom) are known from
this area. A split baluster or reeded decoration on a West
Country top can sometimes be seen repeated in the base; or a
carved motif is echoed in the design of top and bottom halves,
another useful clue that the two pieces are original partners.
Late Georgian and early Victorian Irish dressers were often
made in one piece; another Irish fad was for the 'chicken coop'
style: the base of the dresser has a slatted front, rather like a
cage, for that is precisely what it was. Recently a Gothic style
chicken coop dresser was on sale for nearly £900. Not only was
this a rare and original item, but it was exceptionally well
made, probably for the farmer himself, rather than one of his
workers.

Scotland, the Midlands, Lancashire and Yorkshire may have
produced 'complete' dressers, but it is rare to find them. More
often, the top has been made up at a later date. Other typically
Northern clues are chamfering of doors and glass handles —
though handles, in brass, china, or plain wood, would come and
go with fashion. A single handle lost in transit might well mean
that all the handles on a chest would need to be replaced.

Carving may well reveal the county of origin: Lancashire is
known for a grape and fruit motif; Yorkshire dressers sometimes boast deeply carved backboards. The Scottish craftsmen,
with material to spare, were inclined to use wood lavishly. The

best pine furniture has good crisp dove-tailing, while some of the earliest pieces are pegged. Similarity of structure, wood, even the nails, may all help you tell whether the parts are original or the result of a later mating — a 'marriage'. The marriage might, of course, date from only a few years after the initial structure; then it becomes a matter of deciding whether it is of the period, whether the marriage is a success, and so on. Certain areas, such as the Fens, noted for diminutive cottages, sometimes yield a chest of drawers which appears to have been cleanly cut in half. This could have enabled a bulky item to be taken upstairs and put together once it was up there.

It should not be difficult to get the feel of the pine market, and the competent wood-worker could quickly build a collection of good, unrestored pine and do the work himself; fortunately, the paint has helped to preserve pine down the years. No professional full-time dealer could endure so slow a turnover, but the part-timer could also benefit from the bizarre paradox of the antiques world that buying cheap often means you have not bought a fake (not a recent one, at any rate). Faking is expensive work, and this is reflected in the asking price. Replacement parts, such as turnings, drawer handles or bun feet, can all be bought; Van Heflin, an East Yorkshire firm, specialises in this area. Another advantage of a private pine collection is that some of the rarer items — whatnots, small wine tables, prie-dieus — can be patiently acquired and quietly put away while the value steadily improves. Even dealers would like to hoard, as hedges against inflation, milking stools, corner cupboards with barrelled interiors, settles with bacon cupboard backs, glazed bookcases and grandfather clock cases, but they cannot afford to sit on stock. Country pine is the most coveted of all. City pine was always cheaper; it was made specifically for maids' quarters or kitchens: the drawing room housed fine mahogany and walnut. Pine and oak, however, were all the country dweller could hope to own, so the craftsman lavished all his care and attention on this friendly, but plain, wood. The tell-tale signs of old age are cockbeading on drawers, heavily fielded panels, elaborate mouldings, wide backing boards and a lip on the shelves of racks; any sign of detailed work over and above the carpenter's call of duty is also usually an indication of a good vintage. However, whereas the actual wood used can be a guide to dating with town furniture (no mahogany was known before 1730, for example, in Britain, until the West Indies were opened to trade) pine continued to be used, in the country, across the centuries, so that all of the styles known in oak, mahogany, and walnut periods are, sometimes amusingly, but often impeccably, aped in pine. Due to a lack of machinery in the countryside, early Victorian carpenters resorted to older methods of handworking — a practice which continued well into the nineteenth century. So the rule-of-thumb guides to the late Victorian era in town furniture (machine-made nails, machine cut dovetails) do not necessarily apply to country pine. Dating becomes far more a matter of inspired guesswork.

The beauty of pine is that it is so useful. Washstands with wooden surrounds (inset splashback tiles in the later ones) make ideal petite dressing tables. Those with drawers are used as writing desks by the fashionable. Pot cupboards (euphemistically known as 'bedside cabinets' in the retail trade), even without the chamber, are still ideal bedside tables. Kitchen furniture with numerous small spice drawers is also much in demand. Pine dough troughs, butchers' blocks, blanket chests and picture frames (once gessoed) are all eagerly snapped up by decorating home-makers. For as long as antique pine is cheaper to buy than new furniture that nose-dives in value the instant it is removed from the showroom, there is sure to be a lively market and room for the newcomer to make a living.

A disturbing recent trend, however, is to be found in made-to-measure pine kitchens. Where the old pine is obtained from ancient floorboards (one firm bought up an old convent's floor) and then fashioned into mock-period furniture, this is admirable. Where genuine old furniture, however, is cannibalised to fit someone's kitchen or notion of design, this is a great shame. Protective high status has always gone hand in hand with high price, and, as yet, pine does not qualify.

Scripophily - the busted bond market

The rise in value of bonds and share certificates has been little short of phenomenal. Herzog Hollender Phillips & Company, international traders in old bonds and share certificates, say that over a 17-month period stretching from March 1978 to July 1979 the retail value of Chinese bonds increased by over 1,500 per cent. In other words, an investment of £381 in a portfolio of 20 certificates in early 1978, was, by August 1979, worth £6,325.

Over the same period, Russian railway bonds increased by over 640 per cent and Russian cities, over an 11-month period from August 1978 to August 1979, over 400 per cent. In September 1979, Stanley Gibbons predicted that a 4½ per cent Chinese Imperial Government Loan bond of £500, issued in 1898 by the Deutsche-Asiatische Bank, would sell for around £5,000: it came under the hammer for £14,000, going to a British collector.

Below are shown two specimen investment portfolios of defunct stocks and shares for the period November 1978 to February 1980, prepared by Stanley Gibbons, which show the improvement in value of each bond.

A	Price Nov 1978	Price May 1979	Price Feb 1980
1928 Chinese Belgian Boxer $100 bond	30	100	250
1910 Russian Kokand-Namagan 4½ % £100 railway bond	50	150	250
1912 Russian City of Nicolaiev 5% £20 bond — second issue	40	150	200
	£120	£400	£700

B			
1913 Chinese Government Reorganisation Loan issued by the Hongkong & Shanghai Bank £100	20	30	35
1927 German City of Saxony 6% £20 Loan	16	40	100
1910 Russian Kokand-Namagan 4½ % £20 railway bond	10	30	60
	£46	£100	£195

Herzog Hollender Phillips & Company compare and contrast the performance of old bonds and shares with other comparable investments. They say that if the £381 had been invested in the UK equity market in March 1978, based on the *Financial Times Index*, it would have been worth approximately £375 by

September, 1979 — as against the £6,325 from Chinese bonds. Little has come close to high-yielding securities in fact; compare Chinese ceramics (19.2 per cent compound annual growth 1968 – 78), gold (16.3 per cent) and stamps (15.4 per cent).

All the signs show that there have been big killings in the defunct bond and stock market, that there are further rich pickings to be had, and that almost anyone with time and a certain amount of cash to spare can get started. Nor is there any need to be frightened by figures: a lot of people fight shy of the 'live and kicking' stock market for this very reason. Stocks and bonds have an affinity with banknote and stamp collecting, and little enough to do with the headier reaches of high finance. Indeed, the whole point about the busted bond market is that these often handsomely produced pieces of paper have been poorly researched; ignorance is the norm; whereas, in the quoted stock market knowledge and expertise is the norm. Therefore it would seem prudent, and certainly an intriguing exercise, to investigate to some slight depth the possibilities for a money-making venture into this burgeoning market.

Busted bonds and share certificates first started to hit the headlines in around 1977; *The Times* newspaper set up a competition in which readers were invited to invent a suitable, snappy title which could encapsulate the whole of the legend: collecting defunct bonds and share certificates. 'Scripophily' was the winning entry, and this has now been accepted throughout the English-speaking world. Nevertheless, the story of scripophily began, not in the UK, but in West Germany in 1972 when two students catalogued Russian railway bonds and Chinese bonds as part of their doctorate theses on financial history. So Germany, especially Frankfurt, became the early centre for the 'busted' bond market. Soon enough, other money-minded people and organisations were scratching at the surface, and not only for lucrative gain: the historical and pictorial interest and merit of bonds was beginning to be appreciated by institutions as well as museums. Customers in the German market included Swiss private banks, finance houses in Japan, Wall Street brokers, and many others.

In the UK the market appeared to be slow to get off the ground. The reasons are not at all clear; perhaps people felt that shares had been reproduced by the million and therefore could not possibly hold any rarity value (though there are such things as rare stamps, and they were originally issued by the million);

or else those who had had no experience of the stock market felt that this was a topic beyond their reach.

The company that first came to my attention was Non Valeurs Limited. This was the name of a partnership set up by stockjobber John Jenkins and his associate, a stockbroking clerk. In early 1978, after a mere nine months of trading, this small mail-order business expected to show a year's turnover of around £15,000, (They expected to end 1980 with a £50 – 75,000 turnover.) It was not a bad showing, but it indicated little of the true potential in the market. As Jenkins explained, 'Because of our links with the Stock Exchange, the shares we deal in have to be non-negotiable.' This meant that many of today's most expensive and desirable certificates (the Russian and Chinese issues) were beyond the grasp of Non Valeurs, simply because they are, believe it or not, still quoted on the Stock Exchange. One of the principal tools of the trade for Non Valeurs was the *Register of Defunct and Other Companies*, removed from the *Stock Exchange Official Yearbook*. If a firm could not be traced and did not appear to have gone to the wall, then a merger would be uncovered in the records of the Stock Exchange.

Jenkins's set-up began in a simple way, not unknown in the collecting fraternity. They were offered a job lot, some 600 old stocks, and the partners-to-be put in a bid, which amounted to around 30p a share, for what is still low-price merchandise: Mexican Eagle, an American oil company, which apart from the bright colours (reds, blues, oranges, greens) have nothing special to recommend them. They were, however, to form the basis of the business. Stocks were their trade; collecting old material became their lucrative sideline.

As the business began to develop, and their cheap-to-produce photostatted catalogue began to be circulated, a number of fascinating discoveries were made by novice collectors. Bonds particularly were not necessarily issued in vast amounts; it was generally known, in fact, precisely how many had been issued, and how many had been redeemed or withdrawn.

In 1912, for example, a Cahetian 4½ per cent Russian Railway bond was issued, with only 300 certificates in a £500 denomination. The value improved by increments that would make a Russian blanch: March 1978 £30, August 1978 £75, December 1978 £200, April 1979 £350, October 1979 £500, March 1980 £1,250.

The record-holding bond, the one that made £14,000 in the

Stanley Gibbons auction, is believed to have only about seventeen examples in existence.

It helps to have a look at the origins of bonds and shares, to try to understand the differences and unravel the slight technicalities that deter some collectors. Bonds and shares really do nothing more than demonstrate, in a tangible form, that the holder has a bona fide interest in a particular company. It all began when people were attracted to invest in trading companies when the adventurous nature of the business encouraged them to believe that the return on investment would be swift and sensational. The idea of contributing capital into a common pool and of sharing profits and losses is no recent phenomenon: the system emerged as far back as the reign of Henry VIII. The first company formed on a genuine joint-stock basis, the first British charter company, was the Russia (sometimes called Muscovy) Company, created in 1553. The aim of the company was to open up the 'unknown lands in the north'. Its full nomenclature was 'The Merchant Adventurers of England for the Discovery of Lands, Territories, Isles, Dominions and Seignories unknown'. The company's successful voyage to the White Sea in search of a North-east passage was rewarded, for its success, with a royal charter of incorporation with exclusive rights to Russian trade. Tsar Ivan the Terrible granted it many privileges, not least among them the right to trade in Russia with a tax-free status. The astonishingly successful East India Company was launched in 1599 by a group of London merchants intent on opening up East India trade. In the early days, the joint stocks were arrangements which held good for a single voyage only. As the sharing idea proved itself as a viable arrangement, the share subscriptions were extended to cover several voyages, until, in 1657, investments in the East India Company were made on a permanent basis and shareholders could transfer their holdings to third parties.

It is as well, here, to explain the difference between stocks and bonds. Kathleen Wowk, a spokesperson on scripophily for Stanley Gibbons, has written a concise definition and explanation.

'The market is distinctly divided into two sections. The first and most popular is bonds, which are loans secured by assets, issued by governments and companies. Most bonds are "bearer" which means that they do not feature the name of the investor and can be passed on by the owner to another person.

'They are usually more attractive than share certificates and state, in several languages, the terms of the loan including the amount of capital, the bank upon which it was drawn, the denomination of the bond and the interest payable to the bondholder. Attached to bonds are coupons which were cut off and arranged for the interest payments at pre-arranged dates.

'The second section is share certificates which are made out in equal portions and the owner shares in a proportion of the profits. Certificates feature the name and address of the investor, with the serial number and denomination. The majority of share certificates are not picturesque.'

In the late sixteenth and early seventeenth centuries many joint-stock companies were floated. One of them, still quoted today on the Stock Exchange, is Britain's oldest chartered trading company: 'The Governor and Company of the Adventurers of England Trading in the Hudson's Bay.' In other words, it was the famed Hudson's Bay Company, founded in 1670 to throw open the vast trading potential of Canada to English trade. Twenty-four years later, in the reign of William and Mary, a group of city merchants were rewarded for their loan to the government by being granted the right to found a central bank; this was no less than the Bank of England, formed originally as a joint-stock company, and incorporated by royal charter until 1946 when it was nationalised.

Together with the outstanding successes of the bond and stock market came resounding failures, notable among them that of the South Sea Company, which was founded in 1710. The 'Merchants of Great Britain' were granted considerable trading concessions in a part of the world owned by Spain and suspected of being hugely rich. As well as being a trading company, it also operated as a financial institution (having been created to rival both the East India Company and the Bank of England) and was determined to rival both in prestige and power. In expectation of vast profits, the company overreached itself. It offered to take on some £9.5m of the public debt. Holders of government loan stock were invited to exchange their certificates for South Sea Company stocks — and there was a rush to buy. In the event, Spain's offered concessions were ludicrously mean. To make up lost ground, in 1719 the South Sea Company proffered a scheme to take over the whole of the National Debt, then around £50m. Holders of government stock were again invited to exchange their holdings for South Sea Company stock. The following year, in the wake of an aggressive propaganda campaign, 'South Sea fever' was rampant. Not only South Sea stock, but other companies had jumped on the share-buying bandwagon, and buying had reached manic proportions. However, by the end of 1720 the 'bubble' had burst. Many were ruined, and the directors of the company sent to trial and their estates confiscated.

It became clear that together with high return promises came high risks. Another famous disaster was that of the French 'Mississippi' Company which also collapsed around the same time, bringing with it ruin to thousands of hopeful backers. So you can see how lowly pieces of paper can encapsulate the whole of a swashbuckling era: adventure on the high seas, famous names and famous falls, thrusting entrepreneurs and national scandal.

By far the greatest volume of company issues emanate from the nineteenth century when the first railway companies were formed. In England, the Stockton and Darlington Railway Company was established in 1825: it was the first public railway and the first steam railway in Britain. Two years later, in America, the state of Massachusetts inaugurated its first railway; it is believed that in the USA alone 9,000 separate railway companies were formed. They were not all successful; unissued certificates are a strong pointer to early collapse. American banks followed hotly, notably the American Express Company, formed in 1850 by Henry Wells and William Fargo. Early certificates will bear original signatures of the founders and their value is enhanced because of it. Then, in the 1860s, Confederate Congress raised vast amounts of money to fund the Confederate cause in the War of Secession. Confederate bonds, too, are today highly sought after in the market.

So we arrive at the 'brand' leaders in the burgeoning defunct stocks and bond market, certificates issued by Russian and Chinese authorities. Russian and Chinese governments not only created issues to finance railway development, but also for municipal purposes. Many Russian cities were boosted by bonds in the 1900s; these are also now covetable items. The actual issuing of the bonds was handled by notable banks, such as J.P. Morgan, Rothschilds, the Hong Kong and Shanghai Banking Corporation, the German Asian Bank, the Russian Bank of Foreign Trade and Banque de I'Indochine. In the event, Lenin warned investors against buying these bonds, promising that when the Revolution came they would all become null and void. So it happened. In China, war with Japan delayed repayment and the Communist government under Mao Tse-Tung similarly defaulted.

Famous swindles are also meat and drink to the bond collector. One certificate of immense interest to collectors is a British Land-Grant bond issued in London, described as 'The Poyaisian Land Debenture Bond ... Under the Hand and Seal of Robert Charles Frederick, King of the Mosquito Nation'. The 'king' disposed of these bonds to would-be emigrants to his 'South American paradise'. The king's description was accurate: the 'paradise' did indeed turn out to be a mosquito swamp. The Poyaisian débâcle occurred in 1853; more recent demises have been that of Investors Overseas Services (IOS), and there is increasing interest among collectors for shares originally issued by the head of the company, 'Bernie' Cornfeld. John Bloom's crashed company of the 1960s, Rolls Razor, may also prove to be the front runners; but only time, and the strength of the as yet barely explored market, will tell. At present, typical prices are: IOS £12; Rolls Razor £5; Playboy £50. Rolls Royce, available for pence, by the way, when the firm crashed, is currently £100 – £150.

Curiosities may also turn into covetable collectables. For example, the Hudson's Bay Company paid its May 1860 dividend in mink furs; a Confederate issue, the Cotton Loan bond of 29 January 1863, was 'tri-valued at: £1,000 Sterling— 2,500 French Francs — 4,000 lb of cotton'. You could actually trade it in for bale upon bale of cotton.

When there is a market with vast and sudden fortunes being made, several things become apparent. First, it is clear that ignorance is rife. Then, because of the enthusiasm of buyers, there must be further, possibly substantial, room for development. Again, there must be room for collectors, dealers and auctioneers to become involved in what looks likely to be an enduring interest. Last, but not least, it is apparent that there are any number of avenues opening up for exploration of aspects of the collecting hobby, not all of which are likely to prove rewarding in the long run. However, here are some that are already being hotly pursued.

Signatures make bonds exciting to collectors. There may already be a premium on certificates printed with the name J. Paul Getty, for example; others of the big wheeler-dealers from Wall Street, like Gould (1880 – 90) and J.D. Rockefeller, will also qualify; Wells and Fargo are names to note; as is the British Jim Slater; the printed signature of Hugh Hefner, creator of Playboy Enterprises, is, in addition, well worth discovering.

Variations may, in time, prove important. Early *Playboy* shares apparently had sexier vignettes than the later examples. The graphic merits of bond and stock certificates have contributed greatly to the current demand. Printed colours, often vivid viridian, vermilion or azure, are rich and eye-catching; the paper may be attractively water-marked; and engravings, where they appear, are, as with banknotes, of exceptional quality and depth (to deter forgers), often with the company that printed them proudly named. A well-known variation is associated with one such printing company, the American Banknote Company. Collectors have remarked that the vignette depicting a steam train on the 'New York, New-haven and Hartford Railway Company' is identical to the de-sign on a Chinese banknote of 5 yuan, issued in Shanghai in 1914 by the Bank of Communications. Similarly, shares in the 'New Orleans, Mobile and Chicago Railroad' of 1910 bear the same vignette as the 1 rouble banknote of the Russo-Asiatic Bank of 1917. Evidently, so much work and skill went into the making of the engraved plates that even prestigious companies were reluctant to use them only once.

Rarity must be a prominent guide to value. The brochure issued by Herzog Hollender Phillips & Company includes a useful catechism of rarity:

'Any issue of 300 or less may be considered rare and those issues of 100 or less, very rare. The lowest issues in bonds tend to be the Russian and Chinese, with the 1894 3½ per cent Gold Loan Second Issue (Frs 12,500 denomination) being perhaps the rarest with an issue of only six. But it is not only rarity which contributes to value, any one of the Imperial Russian State Loans had low issues in particular series, but these have not yet attracted the kinds of price increase seen in the more "established" bonds. It is not only the original issue volume which is important, but also the calculation of how many bonds are still outstanding taking account of the redemption schedule printed on the reverse of the document. Many bonds have, of course, been destroyed, deliberately or by accident, and consequently estimates of the number remaining can be well overstated.'

They can also, of course, be understated; only time and diligent research will tell.

Serial numbers may also prove to be important. There is, it appears, some cachet attached to having a bond with 1 or 100 or some other low number of issue on it. In the case of a share, it may be possible to discover who held that particular share. Possibly this will become, in time, the equivalent for the antiquarian book-dealer of the association copy; we shall see. The original face value of a stock or bond may also help dictate its rarity value. Thus, there were usually fewer $10,000 denomination certificates issued than $1,000 ones. The certificates, usually printed on heavy watermarked stock, may be embellished with a picture or motif to indicate vividly the business for which they were issued: thus there were railway trains, ships, mining scenes, and much more besides. Possibly the most graphic vignettes are the railway issues. American railway certificates sometimes feature pictures of massive engines with vast cowcatchers in front. Kathleen Wowk of Stanley Gibbons says that Chinese and Russian railway bonds are among the most popular. Often they show a detailed vignette of a train travelling along a scenic part of its route. One of the most sought-after English railway share certificates

A handsomely decorated 100 share certificate of the Inland Steel Company, printed by the American Banknote Company and dated 1934.

is that of the Stockton and Darlington Railway Company. Another amusing oddity is associated with the London, Chatham and Dover Railway Company. This company, formed in 1853, must have had the worst reputation for punctuality and service in England. In their war of competition with the South-Eastern Railway Company they became involved in vast price cutting exercises, which resulted in lowering of standards in their tracks, locomotives and rolling stock. Accidents were rife — so much so that the railway was awarded the sobriquet 'The London Smashum and Turnover Company'! Indeed, the company was so remiss that one traveller with a sense of humour dressed up as a child and travelled half-fare. When the case came to court, he claimed that he had boarded the train as a child, but had become a man in the course of the interminable journey. The judge decided it was a moot point and fined him a nominal amount.

The histories of famous shipping companies, like Cunard, and British Pier Developments, are also vividly depicted in share and bond certificates. Piers were originally intended as primarily money-making ventures, with mooring and fishing rights paid to the owners. Brighton Pier, the first English pier ever built, in the 1820s, can be seen in its original form in an issue dating to the 1880s; here a vignette shows how the pier looked before it was damaged by storms just a few years later and came to be rebuilt as a pleasure pier. Many English shares dating to the *fin de siècle* were printed on vellum and have a beautiful foil seal of the company; vellum certificates understandably carry a premium in the market.

Some people with no special brief for stocks and bonds are nevertheless drawn by their interest in associated items. Thus, railwayana enthusiasts are keen to collect; there is a man in the USA who collects everything with the slightest connection with beehives; a German brewery buff who is also in the alcohol business is anxious to add brewing shares to his beer-based collection.

In so young a market those who are actually selling bonds are usually keen to establish that they are, in addition, 'traders'; that is to say that they buy as well as sell. Other buyers include financial and banking institutions who are keen to recapture, for their archives, prime examples of their own sometime issues. Leading traders include: Spink & Son, 5 – 7 King Street, London SW1; Herzog Hollender Phillips & Company, 9 Old Bond Street, London W1; Non Valeurs, 'KNYSNA', Redricks

Lane, Harlow, Essex; The London Scripophily Centre Limited, 5 Albemarle Street, London W1; The St. James's Collection, 28/30 Chiltern Street, London W1; Belcher Associates, 352 Grand Buildings, Trafalgar Square, London WC2; Stanley Gibbons, 395 Strand, London WC2; T. Isler, Edison Strasse 10, CH-8050, Zurich, Switzerland; F. Kuhlmann, Seiler Strasse 15 – 17, 3000 Hanover 1, West Germany; F.M. Sutor, Luetzow Strasse 78, 5650 Solingen 1, West Germany; R.M.Smythe & Company Inc., 'Old Securities', 170 Broadway, New York, NY 10038, USA. One go-ahead company, the Vintage Bond Company of PO Box 14, Horley, Surrey, advertised an attractive framed bond in one of the glossy Sunday magazines. Given the undeniable beauty of certain bonds, others may follow in the footsteps of Athena, Diners Club, and The St. James's Collection, all of whom sell framed decorative bonds.

Some of the companies have already started bringing out portfolios and 'beginner's collections'. Herzog Hollender & Phillips claim that in the eight months up to March 1980 their £750 portfolio has increased at a rate of 50 per cent. With the entry in 1980 of Sotheby's auction house into the market, there has been a rush to discover alternative sources of material. Indeed, the excited collector and the finger-twitching money-makers must all be asking themselves how they can get hold of bonds at their prime source; in other words, where do all of the current professionals get their stock from? When a market is known to be a lively one, often it is not even necessary to advertise for stock: people will find whoever it is who is offering the money.

Scripophily expert Annette Phillips says that immigrants who came into this country before the wars sometimes brought with them large holdings; and if they did not destroy their certificates they may well fetch them up, out of hiding, once they know that there is profit to be made. Another way is simply to advertise. The British advertising journal *Exchange & Mart* (Link House Publications Ltd) is known to be a good medium. Because the quoted stocks (and many of the Russian and Chinese are still quoted on the Stock Exchange) can be bought via a Stock Exchange broker, big institutions are known to be buying in this way. The problem is that quality can never be ascertained in advance. You may be buying in vast quantity, and be purchasing little that is of collectable quality. There are moves afoot to pay off holders of Russian and Chinese bonds in the traditional way. Therefore, the bonds that remain unredeemed, floating in the market, are likely to become still more valuable. When a bond was redeemed, in the past, the odds were that it would be destroyed via a shredding machine. The main traditional holders of defunct or busted stocks and shares, however, have long been the bankers and solicitors. It is believed that banks are now getting rid of their defunct holdings via the outlets for old banknotes: banknote dealers are often fronts for the clearing banks, apparently. Even solicitors, the most difficult clients to winkle out of their shells, are now coming into the open in the wake of vast publicity and the thought of off-loading their clients' bulky shareholdings onto the lap of a moneyed collector or dealer. Nevertheless it is early days for this. It may be possible to attract interest and ferret out some of these dormant and dead shareholdings via the national Press, a bankers' magazine or a solicitors' journal. Those who know solicitors and bankers, or who are themselves of the fraternity, will have an easier and a cheaper passage. So new is the market still that those who buy and sell stocks and shares are disinclined to go too deeply into the sort of quality that makes a certificate worthy of collection: on the contrary, in philately and numismatics condition is of vital importance and has long been closely monitored according to a generally accepted scale of condition.

In their March 1980 sale of bonds and stocks Stanley Gibbons used the following reference works: Crisswell's Currency Series, Volume 2, *Confederate and Other Southern State Bonds* (everything in Crisswell is rated on the rarity value scale from 1 to 11), and Drumm and Henseler's *Historische Wertpapiere*. They also graded their lots, indicating that the delineation was similar to that of paper money, as follows: UNC (uncirculated) = clean and crisp, as issued; EF (extremely fine) = clean, but perhaps traces of folds, almost as issued; VF (very fine) = minor folds or creases, showing a little wear; F (fine) = very creased or worn, but still perfectly clear; FAIR = extremely creased and worn, an item that has seen much circulation.

In Sotheby's first ever sale of bonds and old securities of the world, on 19 March 1980, an abbreviated scale of condition was set out in the auction catalogue: Extremely fine; Very fine; Fine. The catalogue adds, 'These expressions are intended only as a general guide and represent a statement of opinion based on the conventional scale for numismatic items.'

As yet, literature and reference works are thin on the ground. The Germans who opened up the market in the early 1970s produced the aforementioned *Historische Wertpapiere*; this is yet to be translated. Confederate bonds already have a certain amount of literature. The best known Confederate reference work is *Confederate and Other Southern State Bonds* in Crisswell's Currency series. Robin Hendy, former stockbroker, and now head of the bond and share department at Stanley Gibbons has produced a useful little volume entitled *Collecting Old Bonds and Shares*. In association with Colin Narbeth and Christopher Stocker, Hendy has now written a more substantial book entitled *Collecting Paper Money and Bonds* (Studio Vista). Herzog Hollender Phillips Company had printed a useful and handsomely illustrated brochure (free) entitled *Collecting Bond and Share Certificates for Interest and Investment*. The London Scripophily Centre Limited is issuing quite learned little typescript histories, the latest of which bears on the Russian railways.

In so volatile a market it may be instructive to have sight (via a photocopying machine, if necessary) of the existing periodical and newspaper cutting literature to date. Though this is not an exhaustive account, it is certainly an indication of the growth of British reference material generally: *Financial Times* (Andrew Taylor) 18 March 1978; *Art & Antiques* (Mel Lewis) 29 April 1978; *Art & Antiques* (Kathleen Wowk) 14 July 1979; *International Herald Tribune* (Jeffrey Robinson) 18 September 1979; *Accountancy* (Kathleen Wowk) September 1979; *Financial Times* (Andrew Taylor) 8 December 1979; *Guardian* (Nick Cole) 10 December 1979; *Sunday Telegraph* (Deborah Stratton) 6 January 1980. That said, by far the best reference material available are the frequently issued catalogues from the various professionals. When I interviewed John Jenkins of Non Valeurs Limited, back in 1978, I was able to describe the topic, based on the evidence of his catalogue, as a subject which 'even a man on the dole could get started in'. Non Valeurs' latest catalogue still has interesting specimens for only a few pounds. The Jenkins credo (Jenkins and his wife alone now run the operation) is to appeal to collectors, not investors. Genuine collectors ('the type of enthusiast who will spend ten years building up a section of his speciality') are now establishing themselves, and he prefers to encourage these rather than the 'get-rich-quick' merchants. Jenkins believes, in the light of recent events, that a classic 'top of the market' situation has developed. People who unwittingly bought at the highest prices the market will sustain at present find they cannot turn over a profit or, in some cases, even realise their initial investment.

When Sotheby's held their first ever sale of stocks and bonds in March 1980, there did appear to be some considerable falling off at the highest reaches: the previously mentioned Chinese Imperial Government Loan bond was estimated to fetch, not surprisingly, £12,000 to £14,000. However, it was unsold at £6,600. There was some damage and there had been professional restoration. Whether this was the cause of the disappointing result, with so rare a document (only about 17 examples survive), remains to be seen. In other key areas, the market outperformed its pre-sale estimate, in some cases by healthy margins.

Sotheby's estimated that their South Sea Bubble stock of 1729 would reach somewhere between £80 and £120. In the event, it went for £180, but this was well down on a 1979 showing for a South Sea Company share of £700 at auction. The Sotheby's example had been repaired and was described as 'only poor to fair but generally clear'. Did this affect the response? Stanley Gibbons are on record in 1979 as saying that 'In another couple of years, prices will stabilise and the rate of appreciation will fall in line with other proven "alternative investments", such as stamps, at around 15 per cent to 25 per cent a year.

It is estimated that the number of stamp collectors in the world can be put at 15 to 20 million; whereas scripophilists are at present under 20,000 strong. The scope for neophytes must therefore be considerable. To keep *au fait* with the market it would be a good idea to join The Bond and Share Society, 56 The Avenue, Tadworth, Surrey KT20 5DE; write c/o The Treasurer.

[3]
The Importance of Knowledge

The more you know in your field of antiques, the more money you can make. To the profit-hungry antiques enthusiast, information is vital. Take every opportunity to read up on your subject; study every picture you can lay eyes on. Take in auction reports in the daily Press and in magazines, and the market surveys issued from time to time by the major auction houses, such as Sotheby's, Christie's, Phillips and Bonhams in the UK. Not all knowledge is useful; not all the facts you learn will stand the test of time. Nevertheless, a feeling for authenticity, for correct attribution (as far as this can be established) is essentially an organic activity; you piece together a jigsaw of dates, words, and images. Later, with a bit of desk work and a reference book, your discoveries can be organised and the points confirmed or rejected. A lot of the organisation of knowledge takes place automatically, the brain absorbing without effort. You do not have to be educated or 'cultured' to know about antiques. Many of the most successful dealers are surprisingly unknowledgeable people. Ah, but they know their subject, you say! Not necessarily. They know what needs to be known; they discard what is not *useful* information. Try it and see; test your local dealer on dates, for example. The Regency period, strictly speaking 1811 – 20, foxes many pundits who will often give a later than accurate date. One thing you can be sure of is that professionals and successful semi-professionals know enough to make money. Let that be your goal; would-be connoisseurs must look outside the pages of this book.

Detective work is a vital part of training. People who have acquired knowledge of antiques over the years, patiently and painfully perhaps, call it experience. There is no substitute for that. Nevertheless, you can quickly acquire a 'feel' for antiques, through visiting antiques shops, museums and country houses furnished with antiques, and through touching and examining items — as far as this is allowed. Often the rarely glimpsed underside of furniture or the inside of a box will yield clues to dating and provenance.

Literature on antiques

Books are of course your main source of information. There has never been so much written about antiques. There are picture books, price guides, monographs, encyclopaedias of antiques, dictionaries of antiques, and more. Which shall you choose? Look at everything, study some works, but buy little because antiques books cost money, sometimes a considerable amount; and your cash is best spent on items, stock you can turn over for a profit.

Once upon a time, books on antiques were compendiums of knowledge: perhaps a dozen or twenty subjects were included, each with a few black and white photographs, each topic polished off in a few thousand words. Today many such works have themselves become collectable items; the antiques they dealt with so casually have now soared in price, rocketing out of the reach of the average collector or dealer. A piece of furniture that could be comfortably purchased in the 1930s for £100 may now be barely within the budget of a major museum.

The recent publishing trend has been towards specialisation, with the subject becoming more and more rarified. Thus a book appears on printed ephemera; the next volume is on an aspect of ephemera, such as printed advertising; and finally a book is written on the advertising ephemera of a single product. As a general rule, the narrower the focus the more worthwhile the book to the serious collector and dealer. For it follows that a writer who produces 40,000 words about the whole range of a collectable must go deeper into his subject if he is required to run to the same number of words on an aspect of that topic.

How do you get to know about all the new books which are published on antiques and collecting? Ideally you would look up the names of publishers who specialise in producing books on antiques in a volume like Cassell and Publishers Association *Directory of Publishing* in the UK. Then you would write to the publishers and ask them to send their latest catalogues at seasonal intervals. I suggest a brief letter on headed paper.

To save time, type your letter on a plain white sheet of paper, leaving a blank space for the name and address of the publishing company, and a space for your handwritten signature to go in. Take this master copy together with a large number of personal letter-heads to an instant printer. He will be able to print or photocopy on to your own stationery. You can then type in the individual names and addresses of the publishers to be mailed, using the same typewriter. Only an expert will be able to spot that each letter has not been painstakingly individually hand-typed. Most of the magazines specialising in antiques run occasional book reviews, as do the British Sunday papers such as the *Sunday Times* and the *Observer*, and daily papers like the *Daily Telegraph* and *Financial Times*. The *Times Literary Supplement* is also sometimes helpful with reviews, but tends to have a broader sweep than the claustrophobic (and more commercial) world of dealing and collecting. Thus, you may find reviewed a book about the pleasure gardens of the eighteenth century, but not a book on *jardinières* and planters of that period. First you must arm yourself with some basic books that you can quickly and confidently turn to. The list that follows is totally prejudiced; but these are the books that I always keep at hand. They have rarely disappointed. *The Lyle Official Antiques Review* (annual, Lyle Publications); *A Dictionary of Small Antiques* (Ward Lock); *The International Antiques Year-book* and *The British Art and Antiques Year-book* (annual, National Magazine Company); *The Price Guide to Antique Furniture* (Antique Collectors' Club); *Collecting Antiques* (Country Life); *The Antique Buyer's Dictionary of Names* (Pan); *The Antique Collector's Illustrated Dictionary* (Hamlyn); *The Collector's Encyclopaedia* (Collins); *The Dictionary of Victorian Painters* (Antique Collectors' Club); *The Camerer Cuss Book of Antique Watches* (Antique Collectors' Club); *International Dictionary of Clocks* (Country Life); *The Country Life Collector's Pocket Books of China and Glass; The Oxford Companion to the Decorative Arts* (Oxford University Press).

These are books that have come my way for a variety of reasons: they are presents, review copies, bookshop finds, and purchased books. You may need other books (my shelves are lined with hundreds of others in addition). Testing books 'in the field' is a time-consuming and a hit-and-miss affair. There is a short cut, however, that I have never seen mentioned before, yet it is the most obvious and sensible ploy imaginable: ask the professionals. Go to the dealers who must make a living from their trade or go under. What books do they use and swear by? Often, you do not even have to ask and run the risk of a disappointment or a snub (though this is highly unlikely); you can pick their brains merely by looking at their shelves. The books they use as handy reference are often to be seen in the cubby-hole, desk area, or money-taking section of a shop.

Once you know the title of a book, its author, publisher, date of publication and preferably also the price (at a pinch, just the title will do) you can then examine it before deciding whether to buy. The best way to do this is to go to a main library to order the book. Bigger libraries often have a larger, more highly motivated staff, with more time and energy to spend following through the more esoteric requests. In London two of the most useful reference libraries for collectors and dealers are the Westminster Library, St. Martins Street, London, WC2 (tel: 01-930 3274), and the library at the Victoria and Albert Museum, London, SW7.

In the UK, many libraries keep a stock of reservation cards on the desk. Each time you go in take a handful to fill in at home, as you come across new and desirable publications. One side of the card carries details of the book, the other your name and address, and there is a tear-off strip for the libraries' own files. The card comes back to you through the post once the book has been found or purchased. Each card has a handling/postal charge of a few pence. It is a marvellous method of examining lots of different books without having to buy. If your library has no such system, suggest that they start one. If your cards amount to £1 or more, ask for a receipt. This is tax-deductible, as is the purchase price of reference books.

New books can be ordered from any good bookshop, though rare is the bookseller who has anything like a comprehensive selection of the latest books on antiques, or even standard works of reference. Harrods in London is usually quite well stocked; and at 41 Fossgate, York, Michael Cole claims to have one of the largest choices of new books on antiques and collecting available in Britain. Send a stamped addressed envelope for a sample catalogue. Another excellent source is The Antiques Book Centre, 93 Bradmore Green, Brookmans Park, Hatfield, Herts.

Often the book you want is out of print, or reprinting. Fortunately there are shops in the UK which specialise in tracing books.

Hatchards Ltd, 187 Piccadilly, London W1;
W. & A. Houben, 2 Church Court, Richmond, Surrey;
Leon Drucker, 25 Dicey Avenue, NW2;
Bibliagora, PO Box 7, Hounslow, Middlesex, TW3 2LA
Hammersmith Books, Barnes High Street, London SW13;
Kent Books, 322 High Street, Rochester, Kent;
Out of Print, 17 Fairwater Grove, East Cardiff.

Some of the most useful books on antiques are American publications. These can also be bought in the UK through a number of organisations, including Quills' International Book Service, 57 Hill Avenue, Amersham, Bucks HP6 5 BZ, and Bowes and Bowes, 1 Trinity Street, Cambridge. For a complete, free, list of stockists of American books write to the US Information Service, Reference and Research Library, 55/56 Upper Brook Street, London, W1A 2LH.

Here is a tip gleaned from painful personal experience. The first thing to do with a new book is to look through it. Turn every page, starting at page one, and continuing through to the end. Do it quickly. Do not read; just look. Even a 500-page book takes little time to leaf through. Merely scanning, the eye notes and remembers almost everything. You will not be able to recall entries word for word, but you probably will register that such a section exists on a particular topic. Having skimmed through the pages, only then should you begin to explore the contents list and appendices. This cultivated pearl of wisdom has been dearly bought; more times than I care to remember I have discovered that the very information I wanted, and which sent me scurrying to libraries and the telephone, was already at hand, in a book that I had not yet fully explored!

As well as books, there are many periodicals of intense interest to the collector/dealer. *Willings Press Guide* (Thomas Skinner Directories), updated yearly, lists many of them, as does the annual reference book, *The British Art & Antiques Yearbook* (National Magazine Company). Some magazines have been going for years (the *Connoisseur* was founded in 1901); others are relatively new, such as *Antique Machines and Curiosities,* a monthly published by Plazbury Ltd, 3 Heathcock Court, Strand, London, WC2R OPA.

Almost every speciality has its publication, many of which are so small and limited in circulation that news of their existence never reaches the standard reference works. However, you may find these small publications soliciting for subscribers or buyers in an advertisement in a general antiques publication; or a new specialist publishing venture may be announced in the diary pages of a general magazine. The following is a list of the main UK publications.

Antique Collecting (5 Church Street, Woodbridge, Suffolk). Published monthly by the Antique Collecting Club.

Antique Collector (National Magazine House, 72 Broadwick Street, London W1V 2BP). Covers antiques, pictures and collectables; gives price or value of the many objects illustrated, and where they can be bought.

The Antique Dealer and Collector's Guide (City Magazines Ltd, 1 – 3 Wine Office Court, Fleet Street, London EC4A 3AL). Monthly.

Antiques (Antique & General Advertising Ltd, Old Rectory, Hopton Castle, Craven Arms, Shropshire, SY7 0QJ).Quarterly.

Antiques Trade Gazette (Langley Press, 116 Long Acre, London WC2E 9PA). The professionals' paper, giving details of auctions and fairs, saleroom reports, and other dealers' information. Weekly, trade and subscription only.

Apollo (Subscriptions and accounts: 10 Cannon Street, London EC4P 4BY; Editorial and advertising: 22 Davies Street, London W1Y 1LH). Lavishly produced and widely respected. Articles on all aspects of art and antiques. Strong internationally — for advertising, and news of exhibitions and salerooms. Monthly.

Art & Antiques Weekly (Model and Allied Publications Ltd, Bridge House, 181 Queen Victoria Street, London EC4V 4DD). Carries features on art and all aspects of antiques for the collector and dealer, including auction and price reports and details of important exhibitions. Published Thursdays.

The Burlighton Magazine (Elm House, 10 – 16 Elm Street, London WC1). Well illustrated articles by international experts on the applied, graphic and plastic arts. Also covers museum and gallery acquisitions, art discoveries, attribution, opinions. Exhibitions and book reviews. Important for international advertising.

The Connoisseur (National Magazine House, 72 Broadwick Street, London W1V 2BP). Well produced magazine of long standing for the collector of art and antiques. Authoritative articles, details of exhibitions, book reviews, saleroom notes. Important for international advertising. (Subscriptions: Circulation Department, *The Connoisseur*, Oakfield House, Perrymount Road, Haywards Heath, Sussex.)

Octagon (Spink & Son Ltd, King Street, St James's, London, SW1). Quarterly house magazine published by Spinks, with occasional 'special editions'. Glossy illustrations of art and antiques, silver, pictures and other splendid collectors' items that the firm has for sale. Free.

Oriental Art (12 Ennerdale Road, Richmond, Surrey; Editorial: 62 Addison Road, London W14; Advertising: The Gate House, Delapre Road, Weston-super-Mare, Avon). Illustrated, authoritative articles and UK and US sales reports. Extensive bibliography published regularly. Important for international advertising. Quarterly.

Clique (The Clique Ltd, 75 World's End Road, Handsworth Wood, Birmingham B20 2NS). Used by antiquarian booksellers internationally for its 'books wanted' advertising. Weekly on annual subscription.

Clocks (PO Box 55, Bromley, Kent, BR2 8LY; Advertisement and Subscriptions department: Model and Allied Publications Ltd,. 13 – 35 Bridge Street, Hemel Hempstead, Herts HP1 1EE.) Articles on every possible aspect of clocks and watches for the collector and dealer. Well illustrated, with notes on exhibitions and book reviews. Weekly.

Hali (193a Shirland Road, London W9 2EU). International journal dealing with oriental carpets and textiles. Quarterly.

International Toy & Doll Collector (29/30 Frith Street, London W1). A new specialist magazine containing articles by internationally known experts and reports on price and collecting trends. Six issues a year.

The Annual Art Sales Index for the Auction Season (Art Sales Index Ltd, Pond House, Weybridge, Surrey). Two editions, covering oil paintings (41,000 picture prices) and watercolours and drawings. Widely used in the UK and overseas by art auctioneers and dealers, collectors, valuers, libraries, galleries and museums. Published annually in October.

The Art Investment Guide (Art Sales Index Ltd). Art market reviews and summaries. Published tri-annually.

Art Prices Current (Wm. Dawson & Sons Ltd, Cannon House, Folkestone, Kent, CT19 5EE). Gives auction prices with details of the most important lots sold and to whom. Published annually.

Book Auction Records (Dawson, Folkestone, Kent). Lists prices of books, bindings, engravings, maps and other items sold at principal book auctions. Published annually.

International Auction Records (Hilmarton Manor Press, Calne, Wilts, SN11 8SB). Comprehensive annual price guide for over 30,000 works of art compiled from more than 11,000 sales worldwide of paintings, drawings, sculpture, watercolours and prints. Illustrated.

The Monthly Art Sales Index for the Auction Season (Art Sales Index Ltd). Lists prices of 35,000 oil paintings sold at 700 international auction sales. Published in 10 issues during the season.

The Period Home (Period Home Publications Ltd, Caxton House, High Street, Tenterden, Kent TN30 6BD). Has articles on old furniture, upholstery. Issued every 2 months.

Silver Auction Records (Hilmarton Manor Press). Comprehensive annual guide to British, American and Canadian antique silver prices, based on records compiled during the last auction season.

Old collecting magazines are a happy hunting ground to the enthusiast. They cost only a few pence (less if you buy a job lot, usually) but contain fascinating useful information on many offbeat collectables. A copy of *The Connoisseur,* 25p, dated June 1905, had articles on silver toilet services, shoe buckles, royal and historic gloves and shoes. Prices are ludicrously out of date, of course, but snippets of information, not available elsewhere, may be an invaluable addition to contemporary sources.

Old magazines, often beautifully produced, are great survivors; but it is a mistake to be intimidated by the splendid loose leaf colour plates and crisp photographs. Most filing systems will not take whole magazines, so you will need to gut magazines to keep tabs of the individual articles they contain. Cut out the pages with a scalpel-style knife; mark interesting items with a vivid felt-tip pen; if you do not own the publications a photocopy is next best thing. (By the way, newspaper clippings fade and crumble, photocopies tend not to and all paper lasts longer if protected from light.) Then insert in a cardboard 'pocket' file under simple headings: Paintings, Furniture, and so on. Eventually the system will expand to include sub-titles, like Oak, Pine, Watercolours, Victorian Oils and so on.

Reference books in action

Old footwear is not everyone's taste, but old clothes are a familiar part of the collecting scene. Shoes are part of fashion; so why not collect those, too? To prove the point, and demonstrate the latent interest, in 1979 the Craft Council staged a year-long touring exhibition, the Shoe Show, a survey, with examples, of British shoes since 1790. How does the collector/dealer become knowledgeable on a subject like shoes? For a start, the Council were thoughtful enough to issue a glossy, illustrated catalogue to accompany the exhibition; this is well worth acquiring. Then a number of books on motley collectables contain references which are pertinent. *Undiscovered Antiques* by Peter Whittington (Garnstone) has a section, albeit small, on boots and shoes. To go with a display of shoes, you might consider a selection of old shoehorns. The Garnstone book also has a section on shoehorns, as does James Mackay's book *Collectables*. Boot- and shoe-trees are another associated relic. Hand-carved beech foot-shape shoe-trees, bearing the names of cobblers and shoemakers, with a metal ring handle on top of the cut-off 'ankle', look marvellous polished up; these already have a market. Patent shoe-trees must be a worthwhile new area for exploration.

Shoes are a fairly off-beat example, but one that demonstrates the value of knowing where to look. Knowledge not only helps you place, identify and date unusual items; it also impresses potential customers. Many people buy bric-à-brac out of curiosity. Take the bottlejack, a spring-driven mechanical device which came into use by the end of the eighteenth century. It was a kitchen gadget from which was suspended the roast. Underneath the jack was a wheel attached to which there were hooks; the roast, impaled on a hook, twirled slowly in front of the open fire as the clockwork motor in the jack unwound over the course of perhaps an hour. The bottlejack, of solid brass and often emblazoned with the maker's name, looks wonderful polished up and standing on a modern mantelpiece or in a display case. Yet few people know its function, and in a private home it can become an amusing little conversation piece. A potential buyer at your stall or in your shop may also not recognise the bottlejack for what it is. A few words of domestic history gleaned from, for example, *Domestic Bygones* (Shire) may whet his appetite, arouse his curiosity, and encourage him to put his hand into his pocket. So remember: the more you tell, the more you sell.

Some years ago I was offered a large and heavy drop-flap table by a totter in Petticoat Lane. I had just moved and needed a dining table. This seemed somewhat big, however, and it was darker than the rest of the furniture I owned. The man told me the table had 'come out of a castle'. So had a great many fairy stories, I reasoned, and took this with a pinch of salt. The totter wanted £25 for his table, but because he was a friend of a friend we eventually agreed on £22 10s (£22.50) — and, to cheer him up, I bought, for another 10s (50p), a plaid travelling rug that had also come from this mysterious castle.

At that time I knew my main purchase to be a good, solid six-seater table, which took a good polish. Over the years, as my interest in furniture and antiques deepened I began to realise my luck. It was the eminent British antiques expert Arthur Negus who first caused me to appreciate my find. In his book, *Going for a Song: English Furniture* (BBC Publications), there is a picture of a Chippendale two-flap dining table, c.1760. My table is rather plainer than this, but the design (the legs at opposite corners swinging out to support long hinged drop flaps) is the same. Negus explained about the various types of feet. A club or pad foot was the plainest possible foot. A pointed pad foot is prettier, and best of all is the claw and ball foot crisply and deeply carved from the solid. My table had a plain, pointed foot. The elegant sweep of the cabriole 'knee' (a feature the Victorians found disturbing and covered with a table cloth!) was another plus. A carved knee, perhaps with acanthus leaf design, would have been better. My table top did, however, have rule joints (a sophisticated form of edging where the sections of the three-part top meet; it means that the floor does not show through when the table is open and that crumbs do not drop onto the carpet) — another point in its favour, according to Negus. Nevertheless, Negus does not show a table quite like mine. Nor does he mention anything about value — which would not be relevant today anyway.

A cursory glance at the *Lyle Official Antiques Review* shows a nineteenth-century mahogany drop-flap table, also on pad feet, though not pointed, discovered on sale for £125. The sketch is not that clear and one could be misled. However, there is nothing confusing about the photographs in my *Price Guide to Antique Furniture* (Antique Collectors Club). The book describes the 'dark, almost figureless Cuban or Spanish mahogany', and mentions the merit of each part of the three-piece top being of one plank. Mine is a four to six-seater;

a larger example would have been better, according to the *Price Guide*. The date given is 1740–50 and the price (in 1978) an astonishing £700 to £800. *The Antique Collectors Picture Guide to Prices* (1979, Ebury Press) shows a table similar to mine, but with straighter legs and club feet. Only a year has passed, yet this *c.* 1740 example, nowhere near as elegant as my 'table from a castle', is rated a £750 buy. Armed with a 'collage' of information, and a photograph, you can easily corroborate the visual detective work by a bit of comparison shopping around the furniture dealers. Alternatively, you could have a chat with a valuation expert at one of the major auction houses (no charge for advice).

By now it would be a matter of acting confidently, with knowledge; and knowledge, in antiques, is strength. For my part, I have no wish to sell that table; its value is bound to increase, so I will just sit tight and watch the price guides!

Phillips issue a useful yearly table, *Antiques at Auction Survey*. This gives brief hints on furniture, paintings, clocks, carpets and rugs, ceramics and glass, silver and gold, art nouveau, art deco, books, Orientalia, collectors' items and stamps. The sheet lists current 'pacemakers', pacemakers to watch, and hedges against inflation. These notes are the opinions of 120 Phillips specialists: always heed expert advice — especially when it is free!

Phillips, one of the most publicity conscious of the auction houses, also produces two more useful sheets of information: *Interesting Prices* (at Phillips during a particular month), and *A Quick Guide to Sales*. The *Interesting Prices* sheet is a hotch-potch of prices achieved at auction; thus, the latest list at time of writing includes the information that an antique oak rustic milking stool on splayed supports made £16; a pair of early Worcester pickle dishes shaped as scallop shells painted in famille rose enamels came under the hammer for £2,600; and, of intense interest to those who collect and deal in model figures and soldiers, a set of William Britain's Salvation Army band, 1936, made £800. The auction sheet lists the days, dates and times of the day that the various auctions in a particular month are to be held.

Subscribing to all the catalogues of an auction house, or even only those that may interest, is an expensive business: this sheet is a quick and handy guide to the ones that may be worth a visit — or at least prompt the purchase of a catalogue. The latest Phillips idea is to produce an illustrated guide to their auction highlights of the year, entitled *The Auction Year*. The book, which contains details, prices and photographs, many in colour, is a fine example of an auction house taking a leaf from the books of antiques publishers who have had such success with illustrated price guides.

Bonhams offer a magnificent and well-illustrated review, which outlines current trends based on saleroom performance. The *Daily Mail*, in its Monday paper, carries an auction section dedicated to a down-market sale at one of the well-known galleries; the topics covered tend to be collectables rather than heavy-weight antiques. Together with a little history, of things like scrimshaw, potlids, militaria and so on, you will get a mention of key lots. Professionals may be able to get on to the subscription list of *Antiques Across the World,* the rather grand seasonal newspaper (though it is more like a magazine in content) issued by the successful shipper, Michael Davis.

Museums which offer information

It is a well-known fact that many auction houses go in for over-the-counter valuation, which is normally free, and almost always so if they believe you are likely to put the item into a sale. The service does not take the expert long and is a good public relations exercise. Less well known is the fact that many museums will also identify and date items, though they will not put a price on anything, as that is outside their scope. This, again, is free of charge. Amazingly, museums are one of the major growth industries, especially in the USA. There are museums to cater for the most out of the way collectables and triviana. In England, there is a museum of witchcraft in Boscastle, Cornwall, a pipe museum in Bramber, Sussex, and a museum of stuffed animals in Arundel, Sussex. Some private museums, like the aforementioned, are open to the general public; others are not. The Domecq Sherry people, for instance, have a fine collection of old and sealed wine bottles; the Coca-Cola Company has a splendid selection of its own historic and highly collectable advertising memorabilia. A friendly letter, on headed paper, from a serious collector, will almost always meet with a sympathetic response and lead to an invitation to meet the curator or a knowledgeable director.

There is literature to help you locate a museum associated with a particular subject. The Museums Association (34

Bloomsbury Way, London WC1A 2SF) may be able to help. There is an Association of Independent Museums, sponsored by brewers Bass Charrington, located at 18 Lansdown Crescent, Bath BA1 5EX, Avon. Eaton House Publishers produce a yearly *Arts Review Yearbook,* listing museums and galleries; a slimmer and cheaper guide by the same publisher is *Britain, A Fine Art Guide.* The best book on museums, however, is *Museums and Galleries in Great Britain and Ireland* (ABC Publications), a guide updated yearly with a comprehensive appendix which breaks down the listings both by speciality and geographical location. There is also a rather drier volume in hardback, available at reference libraries, entitled *The Libraries, Museums and Art Galleries Yearbook* (James Clarke), and another in paperback, *The Museums Yearbook,* published by the Museums Association. Other museum reference books include: *Stately Homes, Museums and Gardens in Great Britain* (AA), *Museums & Art Galleries in the North of England* (North of England Museums Service), and Shire publish museum guides in their slim discovering series — *Toys and Toy Museums* and *Maritime Museums and Historic Ships.*

Auction news

Keeping up with auction reports may well be essential to your operation. *The Times,* the *Daily Telegraph, Financial Times* and some other daily national papers give highlights of the more spectacular lots at the major auction houses. Occasionally the tabloids include sensational auction prices because they cause the general readership of the paper to marvel at how much money other people seem to have and the potty things they spend it on.

The *Antiques Trade Gazette* carries a certain amount of auction reporting; *Art & Antiques Weekly* features an 'Auction Special' section, usually illustrated, which deals in some depth with an important forthcoming sale. The following 'Under the Hammer' section (usually four pages, with pictures) is a snappy round-up of the auction houses across the country; 'Auction Preview' is a showcase of star lots from upcoming sales, and this is followed by a detailed guide to auctions to be held during the week of publication — a selling point which has turned this lively trade publication into an invaluable tool of the antiques

trade. It is also possible to subscribe to auction catalogues and
to receive the glossy preview catalogues issued by Christie's
and Sotheby's.

Art & Antiques deals with many of the less glamorous
out-of-town auctioneers where, in a house clearance sale, you
may well find bed linen following hard on the heels of a splendid
breakfront bookcase. Sending out catalogues, previews and
auction summaries is an expensive business, and an auction
house that agrees to mail you free information may not keep it
up for long — unless you are a customer of long standing. The
Financial Times publishes an occasional art and antiques
'index' report on the state of the markets, and this is valuable
reading.

Antiques in broadcasting

You do not even have to be able to read to learn about antiques.
The BBC's *Going for a Song* television programme was a huge
success in the UK, with its star, Arthur Negus, becoming a
national celebrity through it. After that pioneering programme
came *Collectors' World*, followed by *The Antiques Roadshow*
filmed out of Bristol. In it, Arthur Negus and a panel of experts
from leading auction houses visited eight towns inviting the
public to bring in their putative treasures for valuation and
authentication. In the event, 6,000 people attended, bringing
with them 25,000 items. Rather more tricky to run and follow
are the antiques programmes on the radio; one of the most
recent shows was put out on London Broadcasting's *After
Eight* programme, which features a Bonhams' expert in a
regular Tuesday spot answering listeners' queries. The antiques
enthusiast listens to anything and everything, watches anything to do with antiques, and reads whatever he finds that
concerns his subject; but, frankly, antiques on the radio do not
appeal to me because I cannot see the antiques under
discussion.

Residential courses

More congenial even than watching television are the residential
courses (some of them very short, just a weekend) at which
paying guests can stay, often in considerable luxury, and

attend the various lectures and identification committees and try to learn more about antiques. Sometimes they are also invited to bring along small objects for valuation. The Imperial Hotel in Torquay has been the location for some interesting seminars chaired by Arthur Negus. Roderick Gibson Antiques, 20–24 Hospital Street, Nantwich, Cheshire, has held two-day residential courses. The course is organised and run by a well-known and established antique dealer from his seventeenth century premises in Nantwich, Cheshire. The two-day course (a monthly event) comprises eight lectures covering: suitable premises and ideal locations; dealing with the trade; what to buy and where; shop layout, display and security; accounts, records, book-keeping and VAT; legal aspects; running expenses and overheads.

Sotheby's have now got together with Trust House Forte both to encourage business into their saleroom and to fill up beds out of season at the Cumberland Hotel, Marble Arch, London. Their antiques discovery weekend in February 1980 included bed and breakfast for two nights, an opening talk on Sotheby's and an exhibition and competition and valuations.

Rather more expensive, but possibly more prestigious, was the course put on by Bonhams the auctioneers in April and May of 1980. The cost of their art and antiques course included the entrance fees to the houses and museums visited as part of the instruction; these included Ham House, Petworth, the Ashmolean Museum and the American Museum at Bath. Speakers included the keepers of Japanese art at the Ashmolean Museum, the Cinzano glass collection, and the art deco and art nouveau collections at Brighton Museum. Bonham's, like almost all the major auction houses, are keen on these 'meet the public' occasions; they favour the open house event lasting a couple of days at which members of the public can bring along their possessions for a free expert opinion. Sotheby's have recently started a similar scheme, this time not in the UK but in Madrid in Spain. These 'discovery events' are meat and drink for the public relations officers of the auctioneers; as often as not something quite spectacular comes to light — Sotheby's cite an occasion when a tiny gold coin proved to be a unique Anglo-Saxon gold thrysma, which subsequently sold for £2,600.

For those whose interest lies more in pictures than in solid antiques and collectables, and who have a year to spare, there is the Christie's fine arts course. The course, held in London,

A selection of eighteenth-century English porcelain coffee cups belonging to Geoffrey Godden, representing the inexpensive starters available at one Worthing study weekend [courtesy of Geoffrey Godden].

under the direction of Robert Cumming, includes instruction on painting, sculpture, domestic architecture, silver, metalwork, textiles, furniture, ceramics and glass. The firm claims their course is particularly suitable for those who wish to make a career in the art world.

Perhaps the best known of the brief, non-residential courses is that run by Geoffrey Godden, FRSA, who, as well as being one of the leading authorities on pottery and porcelain, also runs a magnificent gallery at 17 – 19 Crescent Road, Worthing, Sussex. In 1980 there were seven courses, including a one-day mini-seminar entitled Starting a Collection, and 19th Century English Porcelain, English Porcelain Tea Wares, and a beginners' weekend. Although valuations are not given, students are welcome to bring along problem pieces for identification and dating. Guests are also welcome to buy pottery and porcelain, and there is a sales display including several hundred articles, ranging from odd cups and inexpensive damaged 'starters' to interesting perfect specimens from the leading English porcelain manufacturers. Also available for purchase are copies of many of the modern standard reference books (including at least thirteen written by Mr Godden himself!) and Godden's tape-recorded talks with illustrated supplements. Not only is this a magnificent public relations exercise by an acknowledged master in his field, but clearly there is trade to be done as well.

One of the more interesting residential antiques courses was held in February 1980 in Middlemore, Exeter. It is reliably reported that no-one 'gate-crashed' the course — although many criminals might have liked to, because it was a study seminar organised by the Devon and Cornwall Constabulary. Crimes involving antiques, including thefts, fraud, misrepresentation, and so on, are on the increase. The time was right for an in-depth study of what is, for the lay person, a tricky subject. The aims of the course were clearly laid out in the programme for the week: 'The object of the course is to provide officers with some general background knowledge about antiques and similar property and methods of business within the antiques trade. It is hoped that this will enable officers to obtain better descriptions of this type of stolen property, lead to closer co-operation and exchange of intelligence information between police forces and improved liaison with antique dealers.'

A brief look at the topics covered gives a rare insight into the areas which are currently causing concern; these included coins, 'the Brighton antique dealer', ceramics, silver, watches, orders, medals and decorations, firearms, stamps, furniture and paintings.

[4]
Sources of Antiques

From time to time, it is rumoured that the supply of antiques is drying up. Indeed, in certain areas, this is true. Fine pieces of Chippendale, Carolean oak chairs, fine, signed mother-of-pearl-inlaid papier mâché and Old Sheffield Plate have all been priced out of the hands of the middle-of-the-road dealer. That is not to say that they have disappeared from the scene; merely that they continue to circulate, at a more sluggish pace, at the top end of the market, ultimately finding their way into luxury homes, or coming to rest behind the glass of a collector's display case; some are snapped up by museums, or disappear abroad.

This is not the end of the story, however. Fabulous collections reappear on to the market following the death of a collector or the breaking-up of an estate. Sometimes important collections are dispersed when the collector loses interest in his sometime passion, completes his collecting 'task', or simply moves on into another area of interest. There is no evidence that collectors are going to stop dying or changing their tastes. As one type of antique 'disappears' from the market, so other items will take its place. What was shunned in the previous decade, or even the previous year, will quite quickly become acceptable. Pine was once considered very *infra dig.* by the trade; later it became so much fodder for shipping. Nevertheless, as the supply of 'brown' (mahogany) furniture began to dry up, so the look of stripped pine — perhaps embellished with some gadrooned glass (repro) handles, or a bit of brass — came to be appreciated in the UK. The way to tell when an antique has finally been accepted is to watch out for the imitations. With pine, it started with furniture being cannibalised — a genuine piece of old wood, perhaps a door, being incorporated into a new carcass to make an old-looking corner cupboard, for example. Then came the out-and-out imitations: a few strips of pine that might have been felled the day before decorated with a bit of simple fretwork masquerading as a Victorian spice rack, or a boxy set of drawers with brass corners, described as a military chest. As for antiques being 'lost' abroad, there is already a thriving trade transporting British antiques back from the USA to a now more appreciative market in the UK.

Jumble sales

Jumble sales were once a favourite haunt of antique dealers. I remember clearly an interminable climb to a church hall on a hill in the Isle of Wight. I was late and one of a pair of Victorian oils, Venetian scenes by Charles Cousin, was already in the hand of what appeared to be a mild old lady. I picked up the other picture. She squawked: 'They're a pair. And I want them!' 'Well, they're not attached,' I said, keeping hold of mine, 'and I want this one.' Eventually the vicar came over to settle the dispute. They were a half crown (12½p) the pair, he said, but no reason why we should not each have one for 1/3 (6p) each. Her eyes were lasers of venom. That was in 1968, I believe. There is a lovely twin-masted sailing ship set against the Palace of the Doges in my painting, which must be worth a couple of hundred pounds today.

I also bought a rolled-up sewing kit from the 1920s or so. The best part is the scissors, so much more finely wrought than today's chrome-plated ones. That really is about the end of the story for jumble sales at present. With luck you may pick up something useful or, more often, wearable. Too many people know too much to leave anything but freak finds. I did, however, pick up a pressed glass Victorian ink bottle, a Mason's Ironstone platter and nineteenth-century cut glass biscuit jar with lid. Jumble sales cannot, therefore, be totally ruled out as potential sources of interesting or valuable items.

House clearance

Some dealers advertise boldly 'Houses Cleared'. Clearing a house, usually some mean dwelling following the death of an old person without friends or relatives, is a depressing exercise and not for the squeamish. Literally everything must go, and such houses are not usually in the best of condition. Clearing houses can pay dividends occasionally (under the stiff cardboard base lining of an old leather holdall I found a religious pendant in silver on copper and dated 1830) and some dealers form a 'back-scratching' association with executors to ensure that they get first refusal.

The dealer usually quotes a fee for clearing the whole house, but he may offload the unpalatable aspect on to a more lowly dealer who can sell old tins of paint and standard lamp bases.

Antique markets

There is nothing to beat the flavour of the outdoor market, with its early start, bustle, and the urgency to do business before the rains come down or the lunchtime hiatus arrives and the homeward trek begins. In London, almost all the best buying is done at Portobello Road and Petticoat Lane before 9 am, and at the Bermondsey market (downhill in a southerly direction from

A typical sale, this time involving a banjo, at the Portobello Road antique market in London.

the Tower of London) there is more trading done before the sun comes up than after breakfast when the tourists and other hopefuls arrive.

Some dealers cling to their market stalls having abandoned the shops they once also ran. The acquisition of stock is now such a time-consuming activity that keeping a shop, for many, has become an expensive luxury. They can shed the cost of commercial rates and the often prohibitive expense of hiring a competent stand-in and settle for a cheap lock-up garage to store their wares. The one-off fairs are almost always scheduled not to clash with the major markets, which enables dealers to travel perhaps hundreds of miles and show their Petticoat Lane Sunday best, now rather jaded, to a fresh audience.

The Bermondsey market (still sometimes known as the Caledonian from an earlier location) is the most important venue for professionals. It is not unusual to find Bond Street dealers in weatherproof mufti going the rounds with the runners in the early hours, to reappear later in the day in W1 in pinstriped splendour.

As the lorries and cars draw up, a lot of dealing is actually done in the dark and a good torch is essential. Even the way vehicles are packed is a minor art, with the more tantalising pieces placed up front almost like loss leaders in a supermarket. A glimpse of Georgiana may be sufficient to draw the promise of a roll of non-refundable notes as a down payment for first refusal. Almost everyone deals in cash and a thousand pound wad is a common sight.

Goods can change hands several times in an hour, and once despised or ignored things, such as Clarice Cliff crockery from the 1930s, mechanically fretted art nouveau pot stands or a Victorian brass-handled trivet, are now keenly sought. Read a comprehensive guide such as *The Complete Guide to London's Antique Markets* by Jeremy Cooper (Thames and Hudson) and then go at the times the professionals go and see how it is done.

To judge how far 'down market' many of our markets have become, you have only to look at photographs of typical stalls of years gone by. Just a few years ago there were sets of balloon-back chairs gathering dust in the street. Today a set of four could cost £400 and six can go for £800. Even odd chairs, a perennial time-waster, are now snapped up for a variety of reasons. Anything obviously old is desirable; the Victorian chair is certain to be better made than its modern equivalent; an old odd chair sells for less than a new one; it has a resale value, unlike the showroom model; and you can still sit on it! Whatnots were plentiful once; but if you did not have antiques to display, what could you do with them? Now almost everyone has some knick-knack worthy of shelf room, so any piece of polished, prettily turned wood that could pass as a whatnot goes as soon as it is put on display.

The smart indoor markets are the new emporia of the 'quality' antique; but they are markets in name only. The dealers take advantage of shared overheads and even shared advertising and no longer have to worry about inclement weather. Do not think, however, that the saving is somehow passed on to the customer. The little stands are really little shops with prices comparable with the big ones. Dealers also come to an agreement with a neighbour to look after his stall when he is away and vice versa. In many cases if the dealer could not economise in this way he would be forced further down the line or out of antiques altogether and into some steadier occupation.

Antique fairs

Buying at antique fairs is one of the easiest ways of blooding yourself as a professional buyer. You may see a desirable item in an antique shop but you are not quite sure if the price is right, or if it will really go with your colour scheme. You want to go out and think about it, discuss it with your partner or check it out in a reference book. You do not want to reveal your interest to the dealer, however, as you want to knock him down a bit. No matter how askance you look at the object of your desire he will often know what you are after, and your return visit(s) confirms your interest. Another anxiety is that the object may be sold while you are making up your mind. Decisive buying comes with experience. At an antique fair you can wander off to other stands without any awkwardness and return for a second look or to make an offer. Dealers at one-day fairs have the same attitude as one-day market traders — they prefer not to take gear home, and you will often get a better price at the end of the day.

Buying privately

Buying from private customers is a change from the normal practice of dealer dealing with dealer, which often accounts for the better part of business with perhaps 75 per cent of the trade. Private buying quickens the pulse, but upsets can result.

A customer comes into a shop, approaches a dealer direct, or responds to an advertisement offering to buy. This is known as a 'call-out'. In Cornwall recently I noticed that a shrewd dealer, himself on a kind of busman's holiday, had placed a large card in the window of a newsagent listing his wants and offering cash 'as much as you would get at auction'. Sellers were invited to telephone or visit him at his hotel.

You would be surprised how many gems there are lurking in the unlikeliest places: the man who eats his television supper off an anodised gold tea trolley with his feet on a mock leopard-skin settee may well have a Meissen figurine propping up his pools form on the mantelpiece. Almost everyone has some heirloom or valuable relic and it is the prospect of a find that keeps many dealers going and, incidentally, encourages them, against all the odds, to keep a shopfront with their name overhead. Private people are, rightly, wary of itinerant buyers, preferring to trust a familiar face in a familiar place.

The sensible trader does not offer the private seller the least he can get away with — not if he has any sense. He will suggest a reasonable price that takes into account his own overheads, any necessary research, possible auction costs, and of course his profit. Paying the right price may mean a further visit from the satisfied customer or a recommendation to a friend. Of course there is no need to put the newly acquired item on show and reveal the profit margin; it can be disposed of elsewhere. Nevertheless, it may be as well for the dealer to ask himself if he would be able to look the seller in the eye if his mark-up were to become known.

The hazards of buying privately are numerous. You can buy stolen goods and be brought before the courts; you can buy worthless or misrepresented goods — non-professionals are not all sweetness and light, a fact the dealer is often surprised to discover. Goods bought in a private home carry a kind of cachet: the assumption is that they must be fresh on the market. This may not be so. There are also private customers who know precisely what they have and are quite prepared to sell — but only for about 90 per cent of the resale value. Few dealers are in business for 10 per cent mark-ups. Nor is it unknown for dealers to pretend to be private customers. Where a dealer advertises goods for sale privately, the situation can arise in which two dealers, both pretending to be private parties, are involved in an arabesque of bluff and double bluff.

Auctions

The running duel between the auction houses and dealers will not be easily resolved. The problem is spelled out by *LAPADA Views,* the journal of the London and Provincial Antique Dealers' Association: 'The Auction houses, who formerly took a relatively passive role in the system, that of sales outlets for goods largely provided by the trade, have now taken to approaching the public direct for goods and thereby, to an increasing extent, cutting out the dealer.'

Cutting out the dealer means cutting out his mark-up, and it is understandable, if unforgivable, that as the private buyer becomes 'educated' about antiques he is more inclined to trust his own judgement, learn how the saleroom system works, and buy at auction. Some say that the trade for years has been guilty of using the auction rooms as its wholesale supplier; if so, it is hardly realistic to complain when a member of the public discovers that he, too, can buy wholesale and save money. The advantages and disadvantages of buying from a dealer or from the saleroom are numerous and intriguingly interlinked, as we shall see. Nevertheless, anyone can buy from a dealer by walking in and paying the marked price. Buying successfully at auction is a somewhat more sophisticated operation. The auction houses are, predictably, more concerned about the vendors, who are in shorter supply, than buyers. As the big salerooms, however, make money from both (thanks to the fairly new premium system whereby a vendor may forfeit 10 per cent of the under-the-hammer price and a buyer pays an additional 10 per cent on the hammer price, and in view of the fact that dealing in antiques one is likely to be in one of these positions from time to time it is as well to see what the auctioneers have to say about themselves.

All of the four major auction houses are old-established, to a fault: Sotheby's dates to 1744, Christie's 1766, Bonhams 1793 and Phillips 1796. Transpose Phillips with Bonhams and you have the current pecking order, although there is considerable effort being made to rearrange things. The glossiness of the home-produced literature (free for the asking), lavishly illustrated with record-breaking or eye-catching lots, helps to obscure the fact that there is a dearth of printed information about auction room technique. Sharp-eyed saleroom users will note, however, that Sotheby's vendors have to wait until thirty days after the sale to be paid, whereas Phillips pay up in two weeks. Christie's South Kensington state that 'the majority of articles can be included within three weeks of arrival with payment ten days later'; Christie's South Kensington do not operate a buyer's premium and Christie's King Street make no charge for illustration — the details of an auction room's charges will need to be investigated.

How quickly a lot can be included in a sale is of acute importance. Furniture is easily placed in a general sale, the most frequent event. A specialist item, such as photographic equipment, might have to await a collector's sale — sound sense, as this will attract potential buyers with a declared interest. Nevertheless, it could mean months of waiting for the goods to come under the hammer. Clearly, you must telephone the saleroom to discover the details, such as minimum charges per lot, how much the vendor pays if a lot fails to reach its reserve, charges for cataloguing, photographs for illustration, if any, insurance, and so on.

Most auctioneers will give a free, verbal, over-the-counter valuation without obligation. For bulky items, or in special cases, an expert valuer will travel short distances, free, if you appear to be a serious vendor. Out-of-town travelling is charged and a written valuation for probate, insurance, or house division, is priced usually on a sliding scale according to value.

The catalogue

The most important tool the saleroom buyer has is his catalogue. A catalogue is usually issued a few weeks before the sale. You may be able to get one sent free, from a smaller auction house, if you are a regular buyer or a known specialist collector; the major salerooms charge a realistic amount for the service. Some country auctions charge for the catalogue which then acts as a ticket to the sale. A catalogue from a big saleroom heralding an important sale can be as solidly and beautifully produced as a coffee table book. The smaller venues sometimes settle for photocopied sheets stapled together.

Go through the catalogue quickly. briefly scanning each page. Your eye will register items of interest which you can note later. Then go back to the beginning and read the small print, especially the sections called 'Conditions of sale', 'Standard notices', or some such. There may be a glossary to help you understand how the lots have been categorised, or a list of the books used as reference; a key to descriptive words, such as 'proof' or 'extremely fine', in a coin sale; and other little niceties, like 'All lots are sold as shown, with all faults, imperfections and errors of description'; and 'Immediately the lot is sold the buyer shall … if required: pay down 50p in the pound …'.

Damaged goods can be referred to as 'AF' — bought 'as found'. 'Not subject to return' is another phrase to beware.

The way an item is catalogued is of prime importance, especially with pictures. The clue is in the printed attribution. A painting ascribed to 'Sir Peter Paul Rubens' is one the authenticity of which the saleroom will back to the hilt. A picture merely labelled 'Rubens' is as likely as not a copy. 'In the style of Rubens' is an auction house euphemism for a fake. The more initials and appendages to his name an artist has, the more the cataloguer has room to manoeuvre. Thus a 'Teniers' pictures is a poor bet; one by 'D. Teniers' is more interesting; 'David Teniers' will have the dealers flapping; and 'David Teniers the Younger' might occasion cheque-book-waving apoplexy.

The seasoned collector also looks to the 'literature' which may be included in a description. This usually means one of three things: a reference to a book or an article which mentions the picture or item in question; a certificate testifying to the authenticity of the lot, usually written by an art scholar; or a private letter which mentions the lot. The fact that a picture has much literature is often, but not always, a plus point. It may indicate controversy, and you will need to check out the references. Tread warily with certificates, too. In the Depression art historians of otherwise impeccable credentials were known to have dispensed favourably written opinions for filthy, but much-needed, lucre. A letter, preferably from an important person, is often more highly regarded, since it was probably unsolicited. Further pointers to credibility may be marks of previous ownership.

The very typography of the catalogue description reveals much to the trained buyer's eye. Any lot meriting a page to itself and with a bold heading is considered by the auctioneers to be a plum item. Block capital letters at the start of a description are a good sign. Star lots are often illustrated, though others can be, too, to show the scope of a sale — and remember that the vendor usually pays for the photograph, which gives some room for manoeuvre.

A lot may be listed under the heading: 'The property of...' and there could follow the name of a titled personage, a high ranking officer in the armed forces, a famous person from the Arts, and so on. More mysterious is the strapline, 'The property of a gentleman' or 'The property of a lady of title'. In days gone by, favourite expressions included 'By order of a nobleman' or 'Removed from a mansion in the country'. Snobbery sells, there is no question; however, more important to you is the likelihood that these are goods which are fresh on the market, rather than trade goods like a too-brightly-restored and suspect painting, which may have gone the rounds of dealers and salerooms. There may be a list of previous owners, to which you will pay close attention. The lineage, pedigree, or 'provenance' can greatly boost the price — not least when big names are involved.

At the highest level, a picture may bear a royal cipher, indicating that it once belonged in the collection of a king or queen. Famous collectors of the past similarly marked their possessions, and this, too, can be tantamount to an authentication, given the collector's erudition.

Bargains are found in the saleroom, against all the odds, but a bargain is no more than an unestablished work. Before the true quality can be revealed (and value realised) a vast amount of time-consuming research may be needed. Not surprisingly, when a noted dealer or connoisseur collector is bidding for an unremarkable lot this is itself taken to be an authentication.

Understatement in a catalogue description is sometimes used as a 'come-on' by the auctioneers. They leave out some of the (usually easily accessible) literature, in the hope that the studious bidder, thrilled with his 'discoveries', will be encouraged to pay over the top in the heat of the moment.

The saleroom may issue a printed list of estimates, a range of prices which they expect the lots to attain. If there is no written estimate, ask for a verbal opinion. The price guides are a fair indicator of hammer prices, but they should be used with caution. Bear in mind that the lapse between writing and printing dates may be as much as a year, plenty of time for prices to be superseded in the saleroom. Average prices are also notoriously hard to come by. Who is to say whether a particular price was artifically low because of the activities of the 'ring' (see p. 77), or because a rich collector was determined to win, price notwithstanding?

Some buyers put a price on everything, even the things they do not particularly want. Anyone who needs to stay the length of an auction (and the best lots are often, intentionally, grouped at the end) can often pick up desirable and saleable items for a song. The reason is that even though auctions customarily begin on the dot, bidding takes time to gather momentum. Then there may be a falling-off of interest towards the end of proceedings, or buyers may have exhausted their funds. Quite often the lot which immediately precedes and the lot which follows an important item will get less attention than it deserves, because of the excitement of the run-up and the commotion which follows. The astute auction buyer uses any momentary lapse of concentration in others to full advantage. Never attempt, however, to mark your catalogue before viewing.

Viewing

Viewing can be for a few hours prior to the sale or continuously from several days beforehand. Never buy anything you have not viewed, and at the view take time to inspect the lots that interest you thoroughly . If something is locked away in a case, ask an attendant to unlock it. Always handle porcelain; often a fingertip or a fingernail will reveal a repair which escapes the eye. Chairs should be tipped upside down and scrutinised for too-extensive repair work. It is not unknown for an unscrupulous carpenter to turn one period chair into two by splicing on well-disguised new wood. Make sure you see all the lots: the one you miss could be the bargain. Country sales are notorious for lots that need to be ferreted out, largely because someone has already earmarked it for himself. Ask for what you want to see and pester, if need be, until you are given it.

If a lot contains several items, check that everything described in the catalogue is present. A 'folder of drawings' may contain a mass of watercolours, with no mention of quantity or individual description. If you are interested note the number and the ones you particularly fancy. Things often 'walk' at views. In any case, reassure yourself that everything is present and correct before bidding.

The auctioneer is professionally bound not to reveal the

reserve (the price below which the vendor will not sell). Nevertheless, you can sometimes find out the reserve from a porter at a country sale. The top estimate is often, but not always, about a third more than the reserve. Towards the end of a viewing you may be told an estimate and also informed that you will be unlikely to get it for that price. This could indicate strong interest in the lot, or it could mean that there is already a 'bid on the book' which tops the estimate. Where a client insists on too high a reserve, the technique may be to pitch an estimate on the low side so as not to put off potential buyers.

It is easy to get carried away in the saleroom and bid more than you wanted; this is another reason why it is important to mark the catalogue with the maximum you are prepared to pay.

Bidding advice

An auction was once a fashionable event, an amusing soirée and excuse to dress up and see, and be seen by, the right people. Most auctions today are open to anybody, although occasionally entry is by ticket only. Some of the big jewellery and picture sales still are society gatherings, but the emphasis is nonetheless on business rather than frippery.

Novices have an unwarranted terror of auction room bidding. In spite of those comedy sketches in which a Rembrandt is knocked down to the man with an itchy nose, the normal practice is to make absolutely clear to the auctioneer that you are bidding. Raising a hand, an energetic nod, or a gesture with a rolled-up catalogue, are all normal and acceptable signals. The problems start when you do not want to reveal your interest in a particular lot. It could be that a rival dealer, out of malice, will 'run you up', i.e. force the bidding higher to make you pay more. Quite apart from the aggravation of paying more than you need, it may be a ploy on his part to diminish your funds so you will be unable to compete for a later lot. It is possible at big sales, in London especially, to arrange a bidding code with the auctioneer before the sale starts. A crafty one might be that the auctioneer's clerk is to bid on your behalf as long as you have your spectacles on, but that he is to stop the instant you remove them. Be careful not to drop them! Auctioneers are seasoned professionals and willing to accommondate serious bidders with an identity problem, but a sale is often a fraught affair, and remembering an obscure charade will not endear you to them. Many an auctioneer will aim to clear perhaps ninety lots in an hour, and anything that hinders that progress is bad news. Worst of all, the auctioneer may forget the plot and you could become embarrassingly, if not financially, unstuck. For although you are legally liable to fork up for a lot that is knocked down to you, you will rarely be asked to pay for a genuine error. Conversely, if the hammer comes down and you are still in the running, then say loudly and clearly, 'I am still bidding'. The auction room, like the antiques business generally, is no place for shy people, but the last thing the saleroom management wants is a scene.

Better than a bidding code may be to 'pass the bid' to a colleague who has been tipped off to continue bidding after you have, apparently, dropped out. The disadvantage is that another person is privy to your intentions, and 'chumminess' in this, as in any business, is something of a luxury. It is as well to discover well in advance of the sale how the bidding is likely to advance. The best way is to ask. Until quite recently Christie's, for example, used to calculate their bids in guineas rather than pounds. Normally the bidding steps will be £2 or £3, rising, at perhaps £50, to £5 a bid; in the low hundreds each bid could be £10; in the low thousands £100, and on up to £1,000 per consecutive bid or more. The auctioneer can change his tune, however, and cut the cake as he sees fit, accepting a lesser 'pushing' bid, if it suits him. That said, bidding successfully at auction is not only within reach of wealthy dealers and millionaire collectors: in 1979 over half of Sotheby's lots went for £200 or less.

If you cannot attend a sale you can always leave a bid with a porter, having sweetened him suitably and promised a bonus for a winning bid, naturally. The advantage is that, having gained his confidence, he can use his case-hardened judgement to insert your bid(s) at the most pertinent moment. There are agents who specialise in bidding on behalf of clients, but they will not entertain small-time punters, and their normal commission can rise to as much as 10 per cent. You could also get a dealer to bid on your behalf. An alternative is to 'leave a bid on the book' (to leave explicit instructions with the auctioneer). The risk is that he will start bidding dangerously close to your bid, knowing full well that he has your offer in hand, even though he is bound to let you have the lot, theoretically, for as little as possible, bearing in mind the level of interest in the saleroom. Picking bids off the wall is another trick of the trade that will not be eradicated. Most auction houses turn a blind eye to fictional bids being snatched from thin air to boost the price; some openly condone it. You may be able to detect when this is happening as the rhythm of bidding becomes rather more regular than is usual.

The more you frequent auction rooms, and your face and wants become known, so you will pick up tit-bits of gossip and make contacts which almost certainly will prove useful in the long run. A general furniture dealer who clears out a house and stumbles on a pristine-condition decorated biscuit tin from the 1880s may decide to put it up for auction. If, however, he has met a tin specialist or collector through an auction room or elsewhere, he may well save himself a lot of trouble and expense by going straight to the potentially interested party and trying to clinch a deal there and then.

The ring

As an *habitué* you could also be invited to join a ring. A ring forms when several dealers are hungry for the same item. Rather than compete against each other according to the leaps and bounds that the auctioneer dictates, they combine to buy cheap and resolve the conflict privately and amenably. It works like this. The group elects a spokesman or chairman, usually the most successful or a well-known local dealer, and it is he who bids. Having secured the lot the ring gathers, perhaps in a local pub or back room, for the 'knock-out'. Here the leader auctions the goods once again starting at the price attained at the sale. Say the goods were originally knocked down for £100 and at the ring's auction they make £300, then the new buyer pays out £200. This is divided equally among the members other than himself. He also reimburses the chairman his £100 (which has been paid to the auctioneer's clerk and is all the vendor will receive for his goods). Suppose there are five in the ring; four share £200 — not a difficult way to earn £50. It is not unusual, either, for the low life of the antiques fraternity, the 'knockers' and the 'runners', to haunt the auction rooms with the express intention of being included in a ring. They often are included, simply to pacify them and to prevent them upsetting the applecart by running up the price.

If the goods are of a sufficiently high calibre to warrant it, there may then be a further round of bidding, usually consisting of bona fide interested parties and excluding the hangers-on. Of course the ring is tantamount to a conspiracy to defraud the vendor and as such is illegal, but little can be done to prevent rings forming — even exposé articles in the Sunday

Press have little effect. In all probability, given the public's inattention to detail and mankind's feeble memory, dealers accused of malpractice actually profit from the brouhaha, according to the time-honoured principle that all publicity is good publicity. The best way for the seller to thwart the ring is to see that the lot carries a proper reserve. An amateur who tries to beat the ring in the saleroom can sometimes find himself run up out of spite. There have been cases, also, where the ring's pique has been expressed in other ways — such as a hole in the canvas of a picture, or the stretcher of a chair being 'accidentally' stepped on.

The follower

Another scourge of the saleroom is the 'follower'. The follower is usually a specialist collector. He waits for the dealer to place his final bid and then tops it. The follower knows that if he wants to buy that item from the dealer's shop he may well have to pay double the price the dealer paid at auction. The extra bid is a cheap way of side-stepping the dealer's profit margin. Again beware the backlash of the frustrated dealer. Once he is on to you he can force you up to teach you a lesson. In the heat of the moment it is easy to overpay, so winning a paper victory only.

Buying

The astute auction buyer is as sensitive to the weather as seaweed. Bad weather keeps competition down, and very severe conditions, especially out of town, will keep the trade away altogether. Better buying is possible before a national holiday, at the end or the beginning of the season, and in August for the provincial rooms, as dealers are often taking a holiday.

Here are two reminders for successful saleroom buying. Firstly, priced catalogues have the same cumulative value as a formbook to a man of the turf — but antiques are better bets than horses. Secondly, always mark interesting items with your top price, but be prepared to better it by one bid. It is better to regret having bought than to regret not having bought. Moping over 'the one that got away' has a demoralising effect, weakening that forward thrust that is the essence of successful business. If you feel like a loser, it is easier to act like one. You may make a loss at worst; more likely, if you have bought badly, you will wait to sell and then at a reduced profit. This kind of occurrence, however, is part of the antiques business, and must be accepted as such.

Selling

Auction selling needs to be thoroughly researched by the beginner. A telephone call is the best preliminary step. Describe what you have and its condition. The valuer may say he wants a photograph (they usually prefer black and white prints as the colours can be deceiving) before he can comment. Alternatively, he may ask you to bring it in. For something special he may send a representative to see you. You will need to ferret out all the hidden expenses such as cataloguing fee, photography fee if the item is to be illustrated, insurance, handling charges, how much you may be charged if your lot fails to, reach its reserve and is bought in, size of the commission and selling fee. The auctioneer, having accepted your goods for sale, will want quickly to agree a reserve. Do not be hurried; you may be able to gain an indication of the interest among potential buyers which will affect your decision. A seller can bid for his own goods to better the price but only after the reserve has been exceeded. At Christie's South Kensington a vendor cannot bid for his own goods even after the reserve has been passed; if the goods are knocked down to him, inadvertently, he could end up paying for them!

Normally if a lot is bought in, i.e. fails to reach its reserve, this may preclude auctioning the goods for a while. At out of the way salerooms, however, you can often do a deal with the auctioneer and the goods will come up again in a forthcoming sale.

Buying antiques abroad

Carol Kennedy has written a comprehensive guide called *Buying Antiques in Europe: What to Buy & Where* (Bowker). Read this before you venture into serious foreign buying. It is possible, however, to make a start, to get the feel of the thing, by doing a bit of holiday buying. On a skiing holiday in Andorra I met a dealer who had just come back from a day trip to Barcelona. There he had picked up a silver trinket which, when sold in Britain, would, he assured me, pay for his entire family's winter holiday that year. The instinct to deal never sleeps; indeed it is honed by frequent use, but I would hazard a guess that the divorce rate among antique dealers is higher than the national average.

Provided that you know your subject, even general tips can

be profitable. English watercolours, for example, are less highly rated in France than in England. War relics have mostly been culled from the key battle zones, but in Norway a large stock of German World War 2 helmets was discovered. The government had overpainted the Nazi insignia and were using them! Lead soldier enthusiasts could try Malta, Singapore or India; stocks in Gibraltar were exhausted several years ago. British army garrisons used to import stocks of William Britain soldiers (a London maker who worked between 1893 and 1918) to amuse the children of the locals as well as the offspring of the guardians of the Empire. Spain yields good brass and copper, especially fire irons and door furniture — locks (an eighteenth-century lock sold at auction recently for £2,000), hinges, bell pulls — and good brass mortars (the kitchen, not the military, kind).

The favourite foreign haunt for antique buyers and browsers is the Paris flea market. The market, close by the metro stop Porte de Clignancourt is massive and a good guide is a must. The best of these (in French) is one in the series *Paris aux cent villages*. You may get one from the woman selling accordions and brass wind instruments at 7 Rue Villa Biron. Another good guide, with a section on the market, is *Paris Pas Cher,* available from bookstalls. The bible for Continental antique buyers is the *Guide Emer,* from G. Gillingham, 4 Crediton Hill, London NW6.

Glass by the illustrious French makers like Daum, Gallé and Lalique is often cheaper to buy in France than in the UK. Unusual wood, especially farming relics, are easy to find. The unusual flowing lines of many quite ordinary items would ensure a resale in the King's Road. Period clothes are cheaper to buy in Paris, and anyone interested in selling will be pleased to know that the Parisians are currently fascinated by old top hats, and flea market traders cannot get enough of them.

Another big fad at the moment is printers' letters. Most are hand carved, attractive hardwoods. They can be found either singly, in odd sizes, or in alphabets, complete with tiny slivers of wood for exclamation marks and with all the letters and punctuation neatly fitted into a wooden frame. They were used to print posters. Somehow the French have run out of their own printers' letters and are hungry for British ones.

Beginners in antiques harbour fond thoughts of discovering remote areas where the antique shopkeepers still have pre-1960 price tags, or where private individuals, languishing in ignorance, still have odd bits of Chippendale or an outhouse stacked high with country pine (sometimes they do, but the worms have usually made a meal of it). The dream rarely materialises in the UK. So they venture further afield, across the waters. Westford Mill Antiques of Somerset have already set up trading links with Eastern Europe, and under a franchise agreement they are the sole exporters of antiques from Hungary to Britain. Historical knowledge paid dividends. At the time of the Austro-Hungarian Empire, Hungary was one of the art centres of the world and attracted antiques from many countries, especially French furniture. Could there be other regions where a dealer with international entrepreneurial flair could tie up a market?

Before you embark on your journey, contact the embassy of the country you are travelling to. The commercial section is the one you require. Ask about regulations concerning buying and exporting antiques. The French embassy issues a sheaf of rules and regulations in French. In France you will need to ask for a receipt in triplicate, which is not always forthcoming. One dealer I know buys his goods without a receipt, then sells them to a dealer friend who sells them back to him and provides the correct documentation. Buying receipts costs £100 an item, but certain lines can stand that amount of topping up, once the home market profit is added on.

Always ask the seller what steps you should take to export legally. Always declare your purchase at the customs — though officialdom tends not to bother about items that are demonstrably not museum pieces. The museums of Turkey reserve the right to veto an antique export. In Spain permission must be sought of the *Direccion General de Bellas Artes* in Madrid. The *Beaux Arts* in France vets art and antiques above a certain price level. One dealer found a minor masterpiece of a painting from the 1920s. It cost £5,000, but the seller agreed to provide correct documentation for only £500. The British dealer bargained that the *Beaux Arts* would overlook this uncatalogued work and it would slip through. Instead the experts were gleeful with *their* find and, as usual, repaid the cost as stated: £500.

[5]
Methods of Increasing Profit

For years antique dealing was popularly regarded as a scholarly, plodding activity, the ideal retirement occupation. That is not to say that money (even big money) was not being made, even in the country. It was merely that it was not seen to be made, not with any unseemly haste, at any rate, and probably not in the locality. The dealer would quickly take his find (perhaps a fine piece of 'moggy') off to the London salerooms. In the villages, the local antique dealer was a respected figure: he knew about 'things'. He certainly knew about values, for his word was rarely questioned. Since the 1960s, however, the market has undergone a remarkable transformation. Major discoveries in antiques are an increasing rarity; trade frequently depends on a swift turnover, with, often, only a small mark-up signalling the step by step progress of an item from the home of the deceased to the saleroom, to the local shop, to the London dealer, back into the saleroom and on to Bond Street — or possibly to Italy or France.

In addition, television shows, such as *Going for a Song* in the UK, the paperback reference books and the price guides have meant that ignorance is no longer rampant. The market has woken up. There are still fortunes to be made, fortunes are indeed being made; but, as with any big and growing business, and antiques is a massive growth industry, there is a need to operate professionally, to advertise and to think professionally and creatively. Even a one-person concern can dramatically increase his share of trade by applying just a little marketing flair. No special skill or training is necessary; just the ability to learn, and the patience and perseverance to put 'lessons' into practice.

Specialisation

The flexible dealer is the 'long-lived' one; anyone who becomes totally reliant on one small facet of antiques may well find himself out of the market. The argument for specialisation ends when the speciality becomes too expensive, or simply unobtainable. The answer to this is to move on, to specialise in another area. The following are examples of those who have succeeded in their respective special fields of antiques.

Carpets - Robert Bailey

Robert Bailey served for nine years at the largest bonded oriental carpet warehouse in the world; there he learnt about carpets from Persian, Armenian, Indian and European experts. Today his unique operation features a 'bring it to your door' service. He drives the length and breadth of the UK in a Mercedes truck, carrying 400 rugs and carpets. 'There's no obligation to buy; it's an old fashioned service. I tell them the story behind my rugs, and my invoices give the knot density, type of knot, yarn used, and so on. By the time a customer decides to buy he will know as much about the rug as I do.' That could be as much as a week — for shrewd Robert Bailey knows that people get attached to possessions, so he lets them try their carpets for a week without obligation. He also runs a 24-hour answering service, and carpet teach-ins at leading hotels. At the County Antique Dealers' Fair at Carlton Tower in March 1979 he was awarded the White Rose Award by the Duke of Norfolk for the best stand. His next step was a rather more orthodox one: he opened a city store, near Petticoat Lane, to take advantage of Sunday trading.

Jardinières - Barrie Quinn

Barrie Quinn has made a name for himself as the foremost dealer in *jardinières*, planters, and antique pots. Fine two-piece *jardinières* are increasingly hard to obtain. To advertise his shop, Barrie Quinn Antiques, in London's New King's Road, Barrie Quinn had the smart idea to ask *Art & Antiques* magazine if he could reproduce in facsimile form an article the magazine had written on *jardinières* and use it as part of his own publicity. The article mentioned Mr Quinn, of course, but it was essentially an interesting and useful record for the *jardinières* fancier.

Wootton desks

In the late 1970s a dealer advertised for Wootton desks. These are the magnificently Gothic desks, which were a standard fitting in the offices of the Wells Fargo company of America in the age of the Wild West. They look rather like a roll-top desk, but the curved front section, in two halves, is solid wood. The two segments fold back to reveal a flat writing surface, and each of the rounded 'doors' is divided up, on the inside, into pigeon-hole compartments. The Wootton desk is a magnificently ugly piece of Victoriana, but also a useful one. The dealer offered £1,000 cash for the desks, and the advertisements appeared regularly. As advertising in a national newspaper is not cheap, this was a sure sign that he was getting a response. Although £1,000 is not an inconsiderable amount of money, it did not take long for owners (and rival dealers) to notice that when Wootton desks came up at auction they were consistently realising £3,000 plus. No wonder that dealer was able to offer £1,000 cash, and no wonder the advertisements eventually disappeared; most likely the market 'woke up' before it became exhausted.

The similar idea of showing a line drawing of a particular antique, and inviting sellers to do a deal, is relatively rare in antiques, although occasionally an advertisement appears with a sketch of a grandfather clock and the 'come on', 'do you have a clock like this?' There is reason to believe that certain areas of the antique business will need to become conversant with even more sophisticated methods of marketing and selling if they are to survive and prosper in the 1980s.

Cigarette cards

Some people are already doing just that. In the *Sunday Times* magazine in January 1980, Foster-Callear, the direct response merchandising people, were offering, through the post, framed and mounted genuine pre-World War 2 cigarette cards. The cards, issued by John Player & Sons and W.D. & H.O. Wills, feature cycling scenes, film stars, wild flowers, cricketers, footballers, and military uniforms. Readers were invited to buy a frame containing a half set (25 cards) or two frames for the complete set of 50 cards. The cards were hand-mounted and set in a hand-polished, hardwood frame. The delivery price per frame was £18.50, £36 for two frames. The hand-polished hardwood frame would itself cost £8 or £10 retail. The advertising space cost somewhere between £5,200 and £6,400 at the standard rate. As a rule of thumb, turnover must exceed four and a half times the cost of advertising to make a profit; not less than £23,400 worth of orders, in other words. That is a lot of business needed, and a lot of confidence. It also means that vast stocks must be available — 1,265 frames (containing 31,625 cigarette cards) or so if frames are bought singly.

Nevertheless, what a marvellous way to sell cigarette cards! By framing the cards the decorative possibilities are immediately apparent, even to people who had never considered cigarette cards as a hobby. Not many collectables lend themselves to mass marketing; ephemera (throwaway pieces of paper) perhaps least of all. Consider this, however. Suppose one were to corner a particular type of antique or collectable; it might well be possible then to make use of some of the techniques of mail order to reach an elusive market. It is a fact that bottles, Goss, corkscrews, decanter labels, woodworking tools, books, bookplates and even watercolours are sold through the post. The great advantage is that there is no need to visit the seller to buy. Offset against this are the attendant problems of any mail order operation: high cost of postage, insurance, breakages, returned goods, expensive advertising, printing, packaging, continuing source of supply, and so on. Nevertheless, there is scope for the enterprising newcomer to set up a small operation, without need of business premises, vast capital or staff.

Irons - Christopher Bangs

Christopher Bangs specialises in antique smoothing irons. A dozen or so years ago he was not involved with antiques; he was a disc jockey, with a problem — how to store his hundreds of records. A couple of old tailor's smoothing irons made useful bookend-style props. Soon, to accommodate his ever-growing record collection, he had acquired twenty irons; and he started to take an interest in the variations. Without realising it he had become a collector. Little had been written about the subject (a good portent for a money-making opening), so Mr Bangs did his own research, learning to recognise goffering irons (a bullet-shaped piece of metal used by the Victorians to smooth out the frills of a dress), box irons and the several cold 'irons' such as the slickenstones (made of glass or lignum vitae) and mangleboards (wood), used respectively to smooth and wring linen.

In the early 1970s, Christopher Bangs went full time into

dealing. Today he deals only from home, and private collectors from as far afield as the USA, Australia, the Netherlands, France, Germany and Denmark are keen customers. Irons go out, singly, through the post, with larger consignments of weighty metalware handled by shippers. Twice a year he issues a list of collectable irons and other items; for, although irons have made his name, inevitably (and wisely) he has expanded his business to include general early metalware: steel, iron, copper, brass, pewter — as well as small antique carvings, treen, ivories, the type of small items you might see in an early furniture shop, and which are easy to store and cheap to deliver. The proverbial business that begins on a kitchen table and grows into a multi-million pound empire is often of the mail order variety, at least initially.

Mail order

These are some of the antiques you could consider for a mail order operation: writing implements, beer mats and labels, advertising ephemera, medals and badges, beer cans, model cars, comics and story papers, corkscrews, fans, old photographs, stocks and shares. There are many others; but a look at why these might be suitable candidates for postal selling will be instructive. None of the suggested mail order items, apart, possibly, from model cars and photographs, is as yet ripe for faking; simply because it would be cheaper to buy the genuine article than to pay the faker! All of these are small items, either flat, as with comics and ephemera, or easy to pack as a neat parcel: even the biggest corkscrew will fit inside a shoe box. With corkscrews, beer cans, beer mats and labels, and writing implements, there is a wide 'catchment area' of interest. A lot of people are fond of drinking and everyone writes; even those who have never considered collecting are potential converts. The newer an area of collecting, the easier it is to become an expert, if you are prepared to do a little digging and library research. If you know, for example, three makers or patentees of corkscrews, the chances are that you know three times as much as an antique dealer who happens to have acquired an odd corkscrew to add to his bric-à-brac. Another tip for success in the mail order business is to choose a subject with subsidiary potential. Corkscrews are part of the larger activity of wine drinking, which could include early wine bottles, coasters, wine

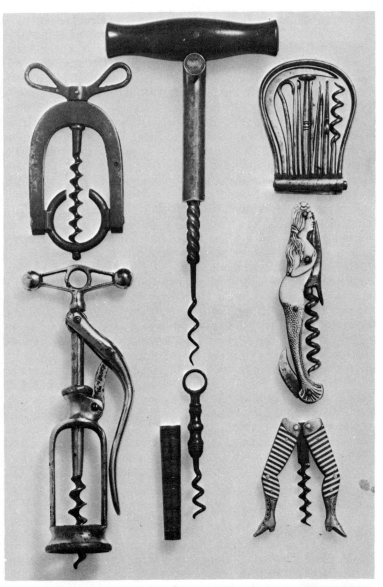

A selection of corkscrews, now becoming a popular area of collect-ables. An individual corkscrew has been known to fetch £300 at auction. Corkscrews, and the paraphernalia of wine-drinking general-ly, are ideal for a low-budget mail order operation.

labels, wine glasses, decanters, decanter labels, and so on.

Apart from stocks and shares, the most recent collectable among my selection, the rest have been collected enthusiastically among *aficionados* for years; but, until recently, they did not attract the attention of the fashionable set with shelf space and a handful of credit cards. Best of all, there may be a society or club devoted to the interest: there is a British Bottle Collectors' Club, an Ephemera Society, and an International Correspondence of Corkscrew Addicts. The organisation as often as not boasts its own magazine or newsletter or at least a list of members available to anyone prepared to join, pay their dues and make the right noises. Such lists (which may include collectors across the world) can be a gold mine to the mail order operator, for people have already declared their interest and are a captive audience. You can save a fortune in advertising to extract the corkscrew collectors from among the entire readership of a general interest antiques publication.

Some of the newcomers, such as corkscrews and writing implements, especially fountain pens, are beginning to make a showing at auction, with the former already fetching three figure prices. By attending sales you may well come to know and meet specialist collectors and dealers, and useful business can result, after the auction, at a private rendezvous. Because 'low profile' antiques such as advertising ephemera and writing implements have yet to make an impact on dealers, and are not well known to the casual collector, there is still the possibility of buying cheaply because the owner does not know what he has. In 1975 I bought a Swan pen for 2/- (10p) in Leather Lane, the street market in London. Its filling apparatus had ceased to function, but the 14 carat gold nib was in perfect condition and the barrel and cap were unmarked. Harrods repaired the filler for £3 and returned it to me, having insured the pen for £6. Today such a pen could come under the hammer for upwards of £20.

Mail order methods

Ease of description is paramount for postal trading. If something is mass produced, like a pen, or produced to a known design, like a medal, cataloguing is straightforward and there is no need for a picture. Your costs rise dramatically according to the number of illustrations needed; so old photographs, essentially one-offs that would benefit greatly by being depicted, would need a substantial profit margin to cover comfortably the cost of reproduction.

Apart from accurate and thorough description, there is a
need to catalogue condition simply and lucidly. If there is an
existing and accepted guide to condition, use it.

Coins are graded as follows. 'Extremely Fine' (E.F. or ef)
coins have slight wear. 'Uncirculated' (UNC. or unc.) is a coin
in perfect mint state. 'Brilliant Uncirculated' (B.U. or b. unc.)
indicates a coin having all its original mint lustre. Only two
descriptions surpass the latter: 'Proof' indicates a coin with a
mirror-like finish, obtained, at the mint, by using specially
polished dyes and flans; and FDC or 'fleur-de-coin' (flower of a
coin), is an appellation which speaks for itself.

What you say in your sales letter, brochure and inserts will to
some extent determine your success, but salesmanship must
matter less with desirable one-off collectables than with modern
mass-produced merchandise. What you offer matters more
than what you say. The following books, the best of their kind,
will help you with writing advertisements and with running a
mail order operation: *Successful Direct Marketing Methods,* by
Bob Stone (Crain Books, Chicago); *How to Start and Operate a
Mail-Order Business,* by Julian Simon (McGraw-Hill, New
York); *Tested Advertising Methods,* by John Caples (Prentice
Hall, New Jersey).

Authorship

Does it help a dealer to be an author? It certainly did in the case
of Bryan Catley of Catspa in London's Camden Passage.
Catley, together with his partner John Sparrow, specialises in
art nouveau and art deco bronze and ivory figurines, and he is
the author of *Art Deco and Other Figures* (Antique Collectors
Club). Not only does he sell the book in his handsome little shop
within the Georgian village, but he also offers dealers a 10 per
cent discount. As well as making a name for himself, Mr Catley
revealed that proceeds from the book enabled him to buy a new
car!

Victor Arwas runs Editions Graphiques Gallery in London's
West End. This is another art nouveau and art deco venue,
specialising in graphics, pictures, sculpture, art glass, lamps,
books, ceramics, and furniture. Editions Graphiques sells to
private collectors, the trade and museums, the gallery's
reputation being doubtless enhanced by the fact that Mr Arwas
is a distinguished author on his subject. One of his best known

works is *Glass — Art Nouveau to Art Deco* (Academy Editions).

Geoffrey Godden, one of our foremost porcelain experts, trading from Worthing in Sussex, does not need to be reminded that it makes sound professional sense to invest time and energy in writing as well as selling. He has written some thirteen well-acclaimed books for the porcelain enthusiast, including *Godden's Guide to English Porcelain* and *Coalport and Coalbrookdale Porcelains*. Mr Godden has gone even further than the printed word, however; he has created a number of tape-recorded guides to his pet topic. These talks, each over an hour long, come complete with an illustrated booklet. There is a big selection to choose, including: Dr Wall Worcester Porcelain, Chamberlain Porcelain, Lowestoft Porcelain, Mason's Porcelain, and Caughley Porcelain. Then there are the Godden teach-ins, six a year, in spring and autumn. There is something for everybody, including beginners, those who wish to consolidate their ability at identification, and even a course for ceramic decorators and artists. There is kudos in becoming known as an eloquent expert; but creative marketing has other benefits, namely cash.

In spite of the name, Nicholas Pine has nothing to do with wood; his speciality is china. Goss and Crested China Ltd is in Hayling Island, Hants. Goss, that remarkably fine, intricately potted, and eminently collectable china, has been accruing in value for many years. People are attracted by the commemoratives, such as Shakespeare's or Burns's house; then there are local landmarks, such as the old court house in Christchurch, a Goss cottage worth perhaps £200. Others specialise in named fonts or crosses, or they collect animals, vehicles, and much else besides. Writing a book is rather like distributing one's own testimonial, as well as handing out a trade card to all those who buy the volume. That, at any rate, is how Nicholas Pine felt when he wrote *Goss China Arms, Decorations and their Values* (Milestone).

For some reason, doll and juvenilia dealers and collectors are abnormally sociable and energetic; they are always to be found involved in events, publishing ventures, fairs and exhibitions. Such a one is Carol Ann Stanton, who like so many other dealers in dolls lives and breathes her subject. Her contribution is as publisher of *Living Dolls and Miniatures,* a quarterly now in its sixth year (details available from PO Box 5, Dartmouth, Devon, England). Helping fellow collectors and dealers to learn more about dolls and keep up to date with doll events is not an entirely altruistic occupation, however; Carol also deals in dolls in Dartmouth, and the more she can encourage the circulation of her stock-in-trade magazine, the more she is likely to prosper. She is also the author of *Heubach's Little Characters, Dolls and Figurines 1850–1930* and a co-organiser of the International Doll and Miniature Fairs which take place in London.

In 1976, Mr M.J.C. Poole was working for Bath auctioneers Jollys. Today he has carved a niche for himself as a very special kind of antique trader. Without a shop, and working entirely from home, in Bath, he buys to special commissions. He is not an agent, and he is not a runner — a foraging buyer scouting out the market for the bigger fish. Most often he will be asked to purchase large items, such as cutlery services, tea sets, or tea kettles on stands. Alternatively, someone with a three-piece tea service may be searching for a matching coffee pot. Mr Poole's go-ahead philosophy, and its successful outcome, has stemmed from the ability to turn dreams into deeds: 'I decided that if I was going to make my fortune in silver it would not be in a shop waiting for customers to come in.' So he advertises in publications like *Art & Antiques* and today he has a world-wide following largely due to glowing word-of-mouth recommendation. Another marketing plus point: he has produced his own publication, *A Guide to Antique Buying in Bath.*

Theoretically, at least, it should be possible both to buy and to sell without setting foot outside your own front door. That is, at any rate, the way Gordon Litherland of Burton-on-Trent, Staffordshire, likes to operate. He buys and sells through the post. Amazingly, his postal business is bottles, jugs, and decanters. Mr Litherland is another dealer who has found that it pays him to put pen to paper: he is the author of *Antique Bottle Price Guide* and *Bottle Collecting Price Guide.*

Shop window advertising

Selling through shop window advertisements is considered to be small time by many dealers. Other more cunning professionals take advantage of the fact that it enables them to sell from home. If they live some way from their shop they probably will not be recognised and can pretend to be private vendors. Selling from a private house attracts private buyers (as well as dealers masquerading as private customers) who would perhaps baulk at going into an antiques shop. In addition, many people feel that the chance of being cheated is lower in a domestic setting, that people are somehow more trustworthy at home. Paradoxically, a dealer will often pay a private person more for the identical object that he would barter for in a market. Ordinary people, unused to such tactics, lose patience earlier, and there is some evidence that, in the 'war' that rages among dealers, the public are regarded as non-combatants.

Shop window cards are an enormously cheap and effective way of canvassing interest in a small locality. In what other medium can you have an advertisement appearing every day for a week for 10p or so? You can even test response to different price levels in different locations. If you offer a pine chest at £15 o.n.o. and a handful of callers are ready to put their hands in their pockets without a fight, then the price will stand an increase, and you can readvertise for £18 or so.

Producing a window card that grabs attention and spells out its message quickly is an art that is easily learnt. Most people do not bother; they do not see that, just as in a newspaper or in a magazine, they are competing for attention with numerous other advertisements. A typed card rates far higher than a handwritten one. Give your card a title (the headline): 'VERY OLD WARDROBE, RIGHT FOR STRIPPING'. Cautious use of red pen is recommended. Do not type in red, but underline in red outstanding details: the price, or the title. A small photograph is an excellent idea: people love looking at pictures. With antiques especially, a picture is worth a thousand words — which is just as well, as you probably have little enough room for a hundred.

Photographs, however, may be beyond your scope, and besides they are expensive to reproduce in any quantity. Drawings are the next best thing. Not a masterpiece of architectural excellence, but a thumbnail sketch that leaves no doubt about the type of object in question. Nor do you need any special artistic ability; if you do not have a friend who can sketch, there are many books to help (the *Lyle Price Guide* is a good one). With a little imagination you could achieve the desired effect. Keep sentences short: 'Original brass handles. Old lock, no key.' Fill the card with copy, around your picture, if you think this will help. The golden rule is: the more you tell, the more you sell. Always put 'only' before the price; and if you are prepared to haggle — and you will do more business if you are — add 'o.n.o.' (or near offer). Many otherwise unbusiness-like people like to drive a bargain in personal transactions; with their cheque (or preferably cash) in your hand, let them feel that they too have won a point.

One week's exposure may not be enough to gauge a response (remember that most shopkeepers will not put cards up on a busy Saturday, your best day for passers-by). Two weeks are ideal. At 10p a week per shop, or thereabouts, you can afford to saturate an area. Having created your paste-up 'master card', with its pictures and bits of typewritten copy attached, draw a box round it roughly the size of a postcard (most stores are not fussy if the size is slightly larger than a standard postcard). Then take the paste-up to a photocopy printer and have them run off as many as you need. Add the red underlining later. Cut out just wide of the line and paste onto card.

Some antique dealers stand a non-descript and weather-beaten piece of furniture outside their stores to show that they are antique dealers and, most important, to tell those driving by that they are open. Manor House Antiques, in Datchet, Berkshire, has an eye-catching and original signal. There is a display of china cats on the roof of this sixteenth-century manor house in which a selection of English and Continental furniture and oriental porcelain is handsomely displayed. Coachloads of tourists on their way to Windsor frequently spy the cats, and Manor House Antiques has acquired a reputation as a local landmark.

Guarantees

Antique dealers, with their traditional fly-by-night reputations, enhanced by stories of old ladies fleeced of their family treasures for just a few pounds, have often found it hard going to convince the public that they were reputable tradespeople after all. Jacqueline Pressman, who runs The St. James's Collection at 28/30 Chiltern Street, London W1, has overcome this problem of getting retail customers to believe in her judgement, probity, and valuation, by proclaiming, in large print, by the entrance to her gallery, that the company will gladly buy back any purchase (she trades in fine art lithographic prints and posters by art nouveau and art deco artists) at the price originally paid — and at any time in the future. Not only does this encourage confident buying at the time, but it also subtly implies that the company is itself confident that prices must rise and that by buying back a purchase they will themselves be able to make a further profit, taking into account the enhanced value of the item over the period of time it has been in the possession of the original buyer.

Even owners of successful antiques outlets are keen to grow, and are aware of the need constantly to reach out, sometimes into unusual new areas, to ensure continued profitable expansion. The following is an extract from a report commissioned by the owner of an antique market. (The name 'Monad' has been substituted for reasons of confidentiality.) The emphasis is not on selling antiques, dealers have that expertise. It is rather on the successful marketing of the antique market over-all.

REPORT ON MONAD'S ANTIQUE MARKET

This report, which is designed to form the basis of discussion, includes suggestions under three headings:

* Special events
* New facilities
* Publicity

SPECIAL EVENTS
The function of 'special events' is to attract public attention, to focus the attention of the media on Monad's Antique Market, to bring more pieces on to the market, and ultimately to attract more paying customers.

Discovery Events. Discovery events have traditionally been held by the major auction houses. The idea is that the public are invited to bring along their (usually small) antiques for identification and valuation by a panel of experts. They may then put them up for auction or in this case sale.

A Sale. Monad's does indeed have a friendly relaxed atmosphere and an appealing casual layout. However, there is a feeling that more could be happening. It is one of those curious facts about antique dealing that an actual sale is rarely seen. And dealers, perhaps by nature or the nature of the business, wear a sombre or even harassed expression. A sale — a genuine SALE — would liven things up. There must be many dealers with goods that just do not shift. The publicity would be a matter of further discussion. Certainly a sale would afford a golden opportunity for effective promotion of Monad's.

A Specialist Sale. It may be possible to organise a selling event that deals with specific items. Perhaps the dealers could contribute to a central stall all their pieces of Scottish Souvenir Ware, Tunbridge Ware, and so on. It would be easy to build an effective advertising campaign that focused on such a collectors' 'special'.

Exhibitions and Displays. Monad's already has a number of attractive display cases. But more could be done with specialist exhibitions. Perhaps the floor that serves as a massive antechamber to the main office would provide a suitable venue. Suggested exhibitions: dolls, scientific instruments, books, militaria.

Or a fashion show. The major auction houses are big in antique clothes. And occasionally a special sale of fashions will be staged. But generally the sale catalogues and the pre-publicity is amateurishly done. It may well be possible to stage, at Monad's, a lively and attractive event in which glamorous professional models show clothes from, say, the Thirties and Twenties — and all for sale.

For further discussion: the possibility of charity shows, seminars, lectures on antiques and dealing. The auction houses run courses on art, why not offer courses for dealers and/or the public on the *investment potential* of antiques?

NEW FACILITIES
Banking and finance. With an ever-growing influx of foreign customers, there may well be a call for an in-house banking facility. Or bureau de change. At least one dealer at Monad's offers Diners Club payment. 'Plastic money' is a growth industry: perhaps other dealers should be encouraged to accept and display credit card payment.

H.P. Has anyone seriously considered the possibility of a hire purchase scheme for antiques? Consider this potentially lucrative market: young couples setting up home. Many would prefer to furnish not with G-Plan that depreciates overnight, but antiques that gain in value and splendour over the years.

An interior design service. Closely allied to the suggestion above, a service that advises on interior decoration, using antiques, fine art.

Investment advice. A pension fund with massive monies at its disposal invests in antiques. Many other businesses and individuals would appreciate advice on investing in antiques. With so many fine antiques at hand, it may well be possible to offer an antique 'investment portfolio'.

Services with dealers in mind. What services do dealers require? What suggestions might they appreciate?

Do they each make private arrangements for shipping and delivery? Could this be handled centrally? It would save time and money. Dealers travel a lot. The possibility of arranging in-house travel and hotel bookings.

Is there a call for professional financial help, centrally based? Such as accountancy advice, help with VAT, and so on. A pension scheme: even dealers grow old. Dealers' cars and vans are essential tools of their trade. What if they break down or a larger vehicle is needed? Possibility of a vehicle pool.

A prestige library. Dealers are avid readers of antique and collectors' literature. They have to be. But do they each need to buy the publications? And many hundreds of books are published each year, many of them essential reading. Could they be available for reference within Monad's in a comfortable lounge-library?

Public/Professional Services. Consider the possibility of a bar or plush restaurant. The bar in the basement of Harrods menswear has become a lively rendezvous, whereas previously it had been merely the waiting room for the adjacent barber shop. A smart restaurant would attract the sort of people who appreciate and buy high quality antiques. It could open in the evening, too.

Music. There may be a case for transmitting subdued classical music in certain areas because of its relaxing effect.

Loan of antiques. There are successful antique businesses that sell no antiques. They loan antiques to film and television companies. With so much stock at hand this could be an interesting and potentially lucrative sideline for Monad's. Often it is the larger more theatrical pieces that are in demand — also the ones that don't sell readily. Here is a way to make money from antiques without ever parting with them.

PUBLICITY
The idea of an in-house magazine is certainly an interesting one and needs to be discussed at length. There is, however, the possibility, in addition, of sponsored publications: one-offs. Books or magazines. Consider: A Monad's Guide to London, which would strongly feature Monad's. A Monad's Guide to London Shopping. A Monad's Guide to Antique Investment. A Monad's Guide to Decorating with Antiques.

Selling 'by remote control'

Because replenishing stock takes up vast tracts of a dealer's time, if he has a shop or a stand in an indoor market, unless he can afford help, or can co-opt a friendly neighbour to sell from his stall in a tit-for-tat arrangement, he is losing out on sales just by being out on the road. Hungerford Arcade in Berkshire has perfected the art of selling *in absentia*. They have some fifty showcases which dealers can rent and in which they display their wares. The dealer need never attend, except to replenish stock and settle up. Instead, under a manager, there are four experienced salespersons who will open the cases, show the goods, and take the money.

One of the more novel methods of displaying and selling antiques on a casual basis is open to people with second homes, usually a house (or cottage) in the country. The idea is to furnish the country home with antiques. In season the house (or flat) is let to people on the understanding that the furniture and furnishings are for sale. The idea is that people become attached to attractive antiques through use; seeing the furniture in a sympathetic light is another inducement to a purchase. By the end of the stay, the guests frequently become so attached to something that they wish to buy it.

A friend of mine has a cottage and she has offered her rooms as an extension for local established antique dealers; they appreciate the extra space and the additional appeal of the domestic setting, without pressure of salespersons or the lack of time to devote sufficient attention to each potential customer. Another boon is that prospective buyers have privacy in which to discuss their feelings — a vital ingredient in many sales. Antique dealers say that the scourge of an otherwise definite sale is when the person says he likes the item but must discuss it first with his partner: this almost always means the sale is lost. As with every kind of selling, a sale should be closed quickly, when enthusiasm is high.

Out of season my friend uses the cottage as a showcase. She advertises in the antiques and national press (the collecting/ personal columns in the *Sunday Times* are a good bet) and when she has garnered sufficient interest, she invites interested parties down, in relays, over a weekend. Invariably, some will let her down; so she makes sure the numbers warrant her own time away from home, so that if some do not turn up she has not made a wasted journey. With experience, she has learnt to judge enthusiasm over the telephone, and has discovered what percentage she needs to invite to be fairly sure of a worthwhile turnout.

Museums

Selling them is just one way, albeit the major method, of making money from antiques. There are others. Curiously, collectors are rarely silent and secret hoarders. More often, they enjoy talking about their discoveries and showing them off. As a collection grows and gains status, however, it can become almost a full-time occupation — without the rewards. One way to profit from a collection, without selling a thing, is to make a public exhibition of it: to open a museum. In America, private museums are a big growth industry. In the UK, free enterprise has a way of getting ensnared by running costs, punitive taxes, value added tax, insurance, and little or no help to be had from local authorities, not even a reduction in the rates (although a museum is often a useful asset in any drive to attract tourists).

Some museum-makers have triumphed, however, against the odds. Cecil Williamson is the owner of three successful museums: the Museum of Shellcraft near Buckfast Abbey in Devonshire, a smugglers' museum in Polperro, and the Witches' House in Boscastle, Cornwall. It was as a collector that Mr Williamson was drawn into the business. When only a lad he became fascinated by pictures of torture. Living in the heart of London's West End, in Nell Gwyn's house, off Curzon Street, he could frequent nearby bookshops and antique shops, which were, then, treasure houses of cheap prints and drawings. Over the years, Mr Williamson amassed a collection of some 6,000 torture pictures, including engravings, Chinese pictures on rice paper (Madame Tussaud's has similar prints, he says; Victorian sailors brought them home from China), and woodcuts. He became fascinated with the study of why people were cruel to each other, and discovered that many of the poor wretches in the pictures were witches. His interest in witchcraft deepened and he began a subsidiary collection, which later formed the basis of the museum.

Today the Witches' House contains Mr Williamson's pictures and much else connected with the practice of witchcraft. There are sacrificial and ceremonial knives, cups for blood, bizarre little waxen dolls, stuck with pins and clad in scraps of clothing stolen from the person who was the subject of the evil-wisher's malice. There are, in addition, colourful diorama, revealing the more intimate goings-on at a witches' ceremony.

Another man who has put his vast collection to good use is Anthony Irving. Mr Irving is the owner and curator of the House of Pipes, in the village of Bramber, near Steyning in Sussex. A smoking museum was not a new idea: the tobacco companies had tried it several times — and failed. Irving, however, had had a unique training: for thirty years he was an industrial entertainment consultant, acting for hotels and clubs. When a club or hotel planned a move into a new area they asked him to predict the type of entertainment that would go down best. At one time he was on call from forty holiday camps and two hundred hotels. Wandering round the towns, discovering what amused people also gave Irving the opportunity to pick up pipes at every junk shop; he says he could fill two carrier bags with pipes for £5! His collecting started thirty-two years ago. Today there are over 25,000 smokiana items in the museum — including over 3,000 valuable historic hand-carved meerschaum pipes and others going back 1,500 years — valued at up to £1m. Irving says that it is the Victorian 'penny-arcade' layout of the museum that is the key to its success (40,000 visitors in 1979, the seventh successful year of operation).

The aim of the museum, says pipe-smoking Anthony Irving, is neither to promote nor to advertise smoking. Smoking has played a large part in our lives, and the paraphernalia of the habit is, he insists, worthy of preservation and display. Certainly the variety of smokiana is astonishing. There are pipes carved in the shape of a woman like the figurehead of a ship, clay pipes galore; pipes made from a crab's claw and a rabbit's foot; a whole case of hubble-bubbles; glass pipes, never smoked but created as a *tour de force* of the glassblower's art; a whole plate encrusted with bands from cigars smoked by Edward VII; a model of Queen Mary built from one match; spittoons; a patent 'Pipe of Peace' invented, oddly enough, by Sir Hiram Maxim, creator of the Maxim machine gun. Irving's painted porcelain pipe collection, mostly from Germany and Austria, is said to be the world's finest.

It was once suggested that he could pick up a handful of pipes and take them to Portobello Road market each Saturday. Without the headache of running a museum, this financial advisor reckoned he could make £15,000 a year. Irving dismissed the idea; he loves the complete collection. His only problem is what will happen to it when he dies as he has no children to carry on the business.

When Anthony Irving bought the premises that now house his pipe museum, he also acquired the adjacent cottage which had been the home of Walter Potter (1835–1918), the greatest taxidermist who ever lived. The ragstone, barnlike building that Irving had earmarked for his pipe display was full of Potter's stuffed animals; and Irving hated stuffed animals. So he sold them to a friend, James Cartland, who in turn set up a museum, Potter's Museum of Curiosity, a few miles away at Arundel. Potter's Museum of Curiosity certainly is curious. It is a 'ragbag' of Potter's many bizarre setpieces of stuffed animals, almost all in their original cases, and a great deal that has nothing to do with taxidermy, too, like birds' nests, an old boneshaker bicycle, the largest shoe in the world (made in leather in the best traditional manner for display at the Great Exhibition of 1851), primitive clubs, arrows, a mantrap, the skin of a giant python and two albatrosses. James Cartland has added to the clutter, with his own superb collection of miniature dolls' house furniture (the finest in the country, it is believed) and his many family heirlooms and bric-à-brac. Other items were donated. When the chimney at the old George Inn in Henfield was opened up two cats, dessicated and mummified in perfect postures of play, were found. Their Pompeii had arrived probably in Tudor times. The cats can be seen today in the museum.

Wilfred Beeching turned his magnificent collection of typewriters into a museum. Beeching had been selling typewriters successfully since 1946; the typewriters (several hundred of them) were housed in the headquarters of his company, Bennett Typewriters. Old and unusual typewriters came into his hands in the course of business, as trade-ins or repairs which he could make an offer on. Now the British Typewriter Museum is housed in Rothesay Museum, close to Bournemouth pier, and is managed by Bournemouth Corporation. A lot of the machines that found their way into his collection were simply swopped for smart modern machines. The Columbia type-wheel machine of 1885 was sold to Beeching for £5 by a lady who used it exclusively for the correspondence of the Dagenham Girl Pipers. The machine, known as the Bar-Lock, looks remarkably like a Dymo Labelmarker; and like its modern plastic counterpart it chugs out just one letter at a time with each turn of the type wheel. Other machines were donated or lent on a more or less permanent basis. For many years Beeching searched desperately for that most covetable machine, the legendary

A Lambert typewriter of around 1896 from the British Typewriter Museum, Bournemouth, originally from the collection of Wilfred A. Beeching. The method is to select a letter and then give the dial a good thump.

Blickensderfer electric typewriter. This American firm was said to have produced an electric typewriter in 1902 — twenty-three years before the pioneers in electric machines, Remington, brought out their prototype. Also the Blickensderfer used a unique type-wheel system strikingly like the famous IBM golf ball. Beeching found one four years ago, in New York, and paid £1,000 for it. All that is wrong with it, he says, is the inking pad. The most important machines are those that were the first to embody a design innovation or improvement or have association cachet: one of his proudest exhibits is the Remington used by Edgar Wallace. Beeching has never lost his collector's enthusiasm, and in 1974 wrote a standard work, *The Century of the Typewriter* (Heinemann). Now retired, he is completing work on another book, on the subject of collectable machines.

Because running a museum can be as wearying as it is rewarding, in 1978 the Association of Independent Museums was inaugurated, to help owners of private museums and to give them a voice at the Standing Commission on Museums and Galleries, which advises the Government. AIM encourages independent museums to become charitable trusts, a status which inspires confidence from would-be sponsors, for then the museum collection cannot be broken up easily. AIM publishes a quarterly bulletin and also organises conferences and seminars on fund raising, marketing and running a museum. (Details are available from The Secretary, Norton Priory Museum Trust Ltd, Norton Priory near Ashmoor, Warrington Road, Runcorn, Cheshire.)

[6]
Money–Makers in Antiques

Jacqueline Pressman

Jacqueline Pressman owns and runs The St. James's Collection, the company name for the antiques and art gallery on the fourth floor of Selfridges in London's Oxford Street. Another St. James's Collection is to be found at Chiltern Street, off Baker Street, London W1. Here Mrs Pressman trades in original fine art prints, specialising in *Les Maîtres de L'Affiche* miniature posters from the turn of the century. The permanent exhibition here also includes the most spectacular selection of work by Alphonse Mucha ever to be offered for sale.

Like so many people now in antiques, Jacqueline Pressman worked her way through a variety of unconnected enterprises before coming into the market. Her success story, full of twists and surprises, offers a refreshing reminder to all those who feel they are somehow not educated enough to go into antiques.

At the age of sixteen, Jacqueline Pressman was not an academic genius. She told her father she would like to go into the arts or the entertainment business. Her headmistress told her father she should leave school at the first opportunity. Immediately after her 'O' levels, and without waiting for the results, she did just that. When the results came through, she had passed all eight subjects; this was the first surprise. It was too late, however, to go back to attempt to rescue an academic career, and her father, a practical man, steered her into a secretarial course at Pitmans. In six months she had successfully completed a nine months' training with such panache that Pitman's offered her a job at head office. She went on to work as a secretary for a variety of people, including a direct selling company and a stockbroker: 'I discovered that I could understand the stock and bullion markets; don't ask me how, I just could. But if someone was doing something that I couldn't understand, I'd ask them *why* they were doing it.'

For a while she worked for a theatrical agent, an experience that destroyed for ever her dream of becoming involved in that chaotic world: 'I found my mind was developing along straightforward commercial lines.' Then she went to work as a secretary-assistant for a man who had the concession for the Rootes Motor group (later to become Chrysler) car sales to the US military in Europe. Aged eighteen, Jacqueline found herself running an office while her boss become increasingly involved with other ventures: 'I had 10 cars and couldn't drive one! I failed the test three times!'

She had no need to know about cars, however; she needed to know about business — distribution, selling and marketing. Jacqueline was discovering that she had the gift of an orderly mind — a must in many areas of dealing where a lot of information needs to be stored and instantly retrieved — and a flair for administration. When the late President Kennedy, in an austerity move, decided to hit at the high life of American forces overseas, cutting their concessionary rights, including their cheap British cars, Jacqueline offered free shipping to America, one of the perks which had been lost. By the time she was twenty she owned the company.

Young Jacqueline was soon to reveal other essential business virtues: the ability to spot an opportunity and the determination and resourcefulness to capitalise on it. A friend, an inveterate 'collector' of potentially marketable inventions, had discovered in his travels across Europe a curious hair gadget, an electric curling tong; it was the prototype of the product now internationally known as the Carmen Roller. Pressman became the founder director of the company which successfully sold and marketed Carmen across the world.

She deduced that this product, which had sat unnoticed, gathering dust on shop shelves, was not being properly promoted. 'A woman needed to be shown exactly what the roller did, and be convinced that she couldn't live without one.' So successful was the marketing strategy that Jacqueline believes a quarter of a million pounds' worth of free publicity was generated, simply because editors were so taken with her rationale for the product, which rapidly became an international marketing success story.

Eventually the company was bought out by a merchant bank. Jacqueline, though still on the board, became less amused by the day-to-day running of the company. She had been travelling around the world, working a seven-day week, fourteen hours a day. With money in the bank, she retired from the hurly-burly; she was barely in her thirties.

One day she paid a call, part business, part social, on the general manager of Selfridges. He was an old friend and sometime business associate. He was worried about the newly out-of-work young lady. 'What are you doing with yourself,' he asked. 'Nothing,' said Jacqueline. 'Now that,' said the man, 'is very dangerous. Your mind is too active. And what are you doing with your money?' She said she was considering the stock market or property. Had she chosen either, at that time, she would have been 'wiped out', Jacqueline now admits. Then the general manager revealed that he wanted to turn part of the fourth floor of Selfridges (after Harrods perhaps the best known London department store) into an art and antiques department. He asked her if she would take the franchise.

Thus far, her interest in art had been confined to collecting as a hobby; she had a Toulouse-Lautrec collection and a collection of miniature carriage clocks. Jacqueline protested: she did not know enough about antiques. True, said the manager, but through her Carmen background she did know about department store marketing. 'He reminded me that I knew about purchase tax, as it was then, returns on till takes, concession sites — the negotiated rate at which a store earns a percentage, and so on.' Jacqueline was intrigued and sufficiently convinced to accept the challenge, and the risk.

Now, with the success of the operation, she understands that she was far better equipped than the ordinary antique dealer. A department store demands a different kind of business discipline: 'An antique dealer usually marks things up if he likes them; I'd noticed, in my own collecting, that if a dealer didn't like something you could buy it cheap. This is fine if you are backing your judgement, but not if you are in mass marketing. It is impossible to specialise in everything, though we do have silver, silver plate, jewellery, art, furniture, clocks and I am heavily into antique engravings and antiquarian books. I realised that I didn't need to know about antiques, I could employ people who were experts: everything we sell is fully authenticated and carries a full money-back guarantee. If we specialise in anything, I would say it was price levels.'

Her customers are drawn from that fortunate wedge of the populace; those with disposable income. Foreign and home private buyers are the mainstay of the operation. When the

The poster by Jules Cheret advertising Loïe Fuller's appearance at the Folies-Bergère in 1893. It is a Maître de l'Affiche poster from the St James's Collection owned by Jacqueline Pressman, who has virtually cornered the world market in Mucha's work and devotes part of her display in Chiltern Street, London, to Maître de l'Affiche posters.

pound was weak, in the late 1970s, there was an even larger than normal influx of foreigners; Dutch, German, Swiss and Spanish tourist buyers arrived on cheap four-day buying junkets. Although the antique trade is little in evidence at Selfridges, there is some reciprocal trading; an exchange of items forms the basis of a deal, and no money changes hands.

Jacqueline's main knowledge is of posters; she learnt about Lautrec, the greatest French posterist, through her own collecting, and quickly deduced that Alphonse Mucha was about to become the fastest appreciating poster artist ever. Posters are only just beginning to achieve acceptance in the art world, she says — though prices are already leaping upwards with the growing demand. The day before our interview, Jacqueline had sold 'the definitive French poster' a Lautrec (Moulin Rouge, La Goulue) to an American dealer for $40,000. The dealer sold it the same day to a private collector for $50,000. Later, another dealer came back to Jacqueline and offered $60,000. It was too late; a professional dealer's word is binding. Nevertheless, she was still smarting from the experience. Why had she not put the poster out to tender? 'Because dealers usually expect you to quote a price; I can't carry on a transatlantic telephone auction.' Apart from posters, Jacqueline now has the confidence personally to buy silver, clocks and bronzes, though when she buys she prefers to go with one of her own experts, not so much because he knows more, but because with her knowledge of buying strategy together they can buy quickly and confidently.

She has made mistakes, and maintains that one of the greatest follies is to indulge a personal taste in antiques. Auction rooms are tender traps for the unwary and unprofessional. 'You have to decide what you want to pay and never go over that; never get carried away. This is difficult when the atmosphere at an auction is designed to involve you emotionally. The only way you can set a buying price is knowing what you can sell an object for, taking into account the 10 per cent auctioneer's commission and the VAT.' The only time you should relax your rigid buying code, Mrs Pressman believes, is when you are offered an especially beautiful item, which you know will not pass your way again. Common sense is one of the most useful watchwords in auction room buying: 'If you know something is rare, and yet you have seen three in a week, and here is another one on the stand, you will suspect something is wrong.'

Know totally your subject, she advises, and specialise. 'Be an expert, be able to see and recognise your speciality; and it doesn't matter how narrow a field you choose. This tunnel vision, as I call it, is the best way I know to make money in antiques. If you could go right through Portobello or Bermondsey markets looking for just one type of antiques you could very quickly corner a market. If you choose, say, carriage clocks, you could start by knowing a repairer and couple of collectors — collectors often know more than the most knowledgeable dealer. Once you know the price you can sell at, then you have established the price you can afford to buy at. With a small capital, taking a small profit, you could comb the markets, building up capital — and knowledge.'

A similar exercise might be possible with ivory or jade; she has less faith in 'gambling, projecting what will become collectable in years to come.' For her own speciality, posters, Mrs Pressman relies heavily on two major works: *The Graphic Work of Alphonse Mucha* (Academy, St. Martin's) and *Das Frühe Plakat in Europa und Den USA* (Gebr. Mann Verlag, Berlin), a book which catalogues every important poster, country by country, but is printed only in German. However, auction records (she attends all the decorative art auctions) form the most useful and valuable record, in the long term. The essential thing is to have price estimates together with the catalogue and prices realised at auction; nothing reveals more clearly availability, and value; nothing is more indicative of trends. The auction houses are beginning to realise this; Phillips produced as a glossy paperback *A Century of Posters*, a glamorous survey of their poster sale of 10 November 1979.

Bennie Gray

Bennie Gray is one of the most successful and best-known entrepreneurs in the antiques business. He pioneered the indoor antique market in Britain, and at one time owned such venues as Antiquarius in the King's Road, Chelsea and the Antique Hypermarket in Kensington High Street. These, however, came later. The first Gray venture was in Barrett Street, off Oxford Street. Gray turned a disused printing works into the first 'antiques supermarket'. It was an audacious christening;

the lure of the chic and the whiff of a bargain rolled into a name; to the trade if suggested quick turnover and a roof over their heads. Instead of the frequently inclement dawn gatherings (not to mention rough-houses) they had grown used to at the Bermondsey Market, Petticoat Lane and Portobello Road, here was civilisation at last!

Bennie Gray has since pulled out of all three operations, not losing on the deals, and has set up several more antique markets. Alfie's in Church Street, off Edgeware Road, just north of Marble Arch, still has the feeling (and to some extent the look) of a Portobello Road with a lid on: the basement boasts a dealer specialising in antique lavatory bowls and bathroom fitments. His two up-market markets, Gray's Market, Davies Street, and Gray's Mews, at either end of a splendid, listed Victorian building, once showroom of Boulding's the plumbers' merchants, are antiques emporia.

Meeting Gray, I expected to find a brash, fast-talking man — especially having discovered that he began in property, learning in a few weeks how to recondition old buildings, and still apparently thrives on the many different crafts that are together needed to turn a shambles into a showcase. This was not the case however. Bennie sits quietly, almost sedately, and does not waste words or movements. Subtle good taste pervades his office, painted vivid green, decked with intricately carved antiques and hung with splendid paintings. Everything, including Bennie himself, is not quite what it seems; it is better. The carvings are medieval; the pictures are from the hand of Lord Leighton; and Bennie Gray is a London University graduate with a first class honours degree in engineering: he turned down an offer of a PhD in gas turbine engines and a promising career in the aerospace industry to flesh out a fantasy: to create a relaxed atmosphere for the antiques fraternity, a place that people *want* to be in. From the dealers' point of view, they are able to relax largely because overheads are low. (The indoor market did not replace the street markets, of course, it merely offered a fresh venue, new faces, another link in the selling chain.)

Customers are drawn in, not least because the price is right, but also because the environment is enticing. Gray worries about the look of a place: Gray's Mews has tastefully-drawn tropical scenes on the walls, thickly carpeted stairs. He senses that buyers and customers want the atmosphere, prices and merchandise to be, somehow, all of a piece. The drive to achieve this aim is rooted in a kind of creative cussedness. Gray claims his real ambition is 'doing the things that displease me least.' 'I wanted not to have to go to work nine to five; and to do that I had to have money.' Thus, although he was 'adept at gas turbines', and he would have got in at the start of rocketry, an exciting prospect for a bright graduate, it would have meant a salary in the order of £10 to £15 a week. It was the mid-1950s; he was twenty-one; and it was not much to speak of even then.

In spite of an early interest in the arts and antiques (particularly in the decadent writers, such as Pater and Oscar Wilde, and in the pre-Raphaelites, especially Holman Hunt and Rosetti, William Morris furniture and the arts and crafts movement generally), Gray did not immediately get involved with the business, but he had long been a collector. 'When I was very young, and had almost no money, I was able to build up a collection of smashing things: fine drawings by Burne-Jones for £5 each, museum pieces now. I was still at school when I started. I did a paper round to fund my buying.'

So the ever-resourceful Bennie Gray began his career selling compressed air machinery. Several other jobs and three years later, with a few hundred pounds in the bank, his more heady aspirations were beginning to prick: 'Rather than saving a couple of pounds a week in the Post Office, I decided to try and make money as an entrepreneur.' He became intrigued by the then novel possibility of buying up an old house and converting it into flats and selling it off. He managed to finance his first project 'by the seat of my pants'. He found a building in Knightsbridge, borrowed a small amount of money from the bank, 'scrounged' a little, and added sufficiently to his hard-won £800 to begin. 'By applying the disciplines and logic you go through when learning a science,' Gray says, he managed to learn in a few weeks how to recondition a Victorian building.

It was the beginning of the 1960s and Bennie Gray had entered the property business. For a while he loved it: 'Being an amateur, jobbing builder is one of the delights for me. I quite fancy myself as a designer, architect, builder.' He also made a few thousand pounds and decided that the time was right, once again, to change course, according to his heart's desire: he was going to learn the piano. There was music in his blood (his father had been a drummer) and here was the opportunity. He went to Trinity College of Music; he practised six and seven hours a day, spending weeks on Beethoven sonatas that others would play at sight. He kept at the keyboard until his fingers bled. It was all to no avail; the time had been right, but the talent was just not there.

On another occasion when Gray had digressed from his apostolic role as the provider of exquisite antiques emporia, he did not come unstuck. He became a journalist, wrote about the hack property developers who were at the time gutting London of its neglected architectural heritage, instead of lovingly restoring buildings as Gray would have wished, and in 1973 he won the IPC 'Campaigning Journalist of the Year' award.

Grade A intellects can, after all, apply themselves to almost anything and succeed. Gray sees himself as a kind of inspired jack of all trades: 'I'm quite good at a lot of different things, and very good at nothing. Setting up a big antiques market, you need to be confident. You need to be something of an estate agent, solicitor, architect, surveyor, building tradesman, building manager, designer. I delegate only the formal side of the business — corporate structure, accountancy. You have to be aware of everything down to the last detail and be there when there's a problem and people need you.'

He describes the antiques trade as 'the only growth industry in this country. More and more people are dissatisfied with the present and frightened of the future; so they look to the past. Antique dealers peddle the tokens of nostalgia.' What got the ball rolling for Gray was his perception of a problem that is endemic to the antiques trade: dealers were constantly short of pieces to trade with; they are also terrified of high rents and overheads, for these are continuing factors which gnaw at capital even in lean times. 'It seemed to me,' says Gray, 'that if a lot of dealers could get together and operate in one building they could afford to be very central.' They would not only save money, he reasoned, but they would also generate more trade.

The first development, in 1964, the Barrett Street complex, was a site due for development; nevertheless, Gray gambled and took a short lease. He drew together twenty-seven dealers, many of them acquaintances, and they each reserved a stand. 'At the last minute I decided to call it the Antique Supermarket. It was an absurd title for antiques, but it captured a lot of attention.'

Attention-getting tactics have been a cornerstone of Gray's success. In 1966 he flew to Dublin to try to recapture Nelson's head, spirited away from the dynamited and decapitated stone Nelson Pillar in O'Connell Street. He inveigled himself into the good books of the thieves, and smuggled the head over the border and back home to display it at Barrett Street. The following year he inaugurated the Hypermarket in Kensington. It was to be the *crème de la crème* trading post, and Gray hit on a visual motif that would instantly and spectacularly put the classy message across. The shop front would feature six caryatids, perfect replicas of those to be found supporting the Erectheon in Athens. As a model he used the best example,

Barrett Street Antique Supermarket, Bennie Gray's first experiment (he no longer owns it) in turning a large building into a covered antiques trading emporium. There are more stands inside and upstairs.

which had been whisked away to the British Museum many years ago. The museum made a cast and this was used to manufacture six glass-fibre caryatids.

So successful was the archaeological sleight of hand that the Greek government, seeing Gray's magnificent duplicates, decided to rescue the remaining pillars from their treasured but decaying heritagé, place them in a museum, and replace them with Gray-style glass-fibre substitutes!

Bennie Gray also furnished the Hypermarket with an Edwardian railway dining car, bought from British Rail. Complete with splendid mahogany trim, inlaid brass and mirror decorations, it became an eye-catching coffee bar. In spite of the promotional ingenuity, however, the Hypermarket never took off in the way the Barrett Street market had done. Perhaps it was too chic; possibly it lacked passing trade, merely suffering the fate of other stores along the Kensington High Street, then a depressed shopping promenade.

Gray applied the same flair for innovation and design to the interior of the latest indoor market, near Bond Street. Here it was discovered that the frequent flooding in the basement was caused by a 'lost' tributary of the river Tyburn, an ancient waterway which runs under South Molton Lane. He could have diverted it and concreted it over; instead, it has become an attractive design feature of the basement. Browsers are able to sit on the 'banks' of the stream which runs the length of the building and gaze at the goldfish. The stream, really no more than a trough of water, has been worth its weight in gold in terms of the publicity it has received.

Creature comforts feature high on Gray's list of business priorities. Davies Mews has a restaurant specialising in wholefood; Gray's Mews also has a snack and salad bar, a bureau de change, a concert area, for baroque music recitals, craft workshops, and more. The Mews also has wall-mounted display cases, so that dealers who are not even stand holders can display their (small) wares and a card saying where they can be purchased.

The thrill of being at the helm of an antiques empire Gray rates more highly than earthly goods — almost. 'I have never been driven to make money, otherwise I'd be seriously rich by now. I'm well provided for, I won't starve.'

Michael Davis

'We're gearing ourselves up to be the top international specialist movers of antiques.' That is what Michael Davis said to me a couple of years ago. Today Michael Davis, specialist packers and shippers, international removers and travel-related services, have handsomely achieved that objective; but where do they go from here? Speaking from his 50,000 square foot warehouse (Europe's largest and most modern packing facility) in Kew, Michael Davis said: 'We are the biggest service of our type in the world, but we haven't really tapped the market fully yet; there's a lot of expanding and servicing, a lot of accounts still to get.'

The essence of Michael Davis' success is that he has never been satisfied with it. In 1972, the year that Michael Davis Shipping Limited began, Davis set out his aspirations in a classy piece of advertising: 'We thought, despite the large number of companies currently in the antique shipping business, that there was room for one more ... we set out to help the overseas buyer in the most professional and business-like way possible. We organise flights, itineraries, hotels and couriers. We meet dealers from their planes. We pay their bills, collect their purchases, organise customs clearance, and a million and one other things. We pack — and then, last of all, do we ship. We understand that to a dealer, stock on the high seas is working capital tied up .... Today, we believe that we are the biggest and most efficient specialist shippers of antiques in the world. But what we believe isn't really important. It's what our clients think that counts.'

There follow eight pages of advertising replete with glowing testimonials from satisfied customers and a further exposition of the multifarious services that Michael Davis offers. When the *New York Times* ran a glowing personality piece on him in 1977 Michael Davis was swift to have it reproduced and circularised among his customers and potential clients. The article began 'Michael Davis has shipped a gypsy caravan to Oklahoma, a Messerschmitt to Atlanta, and the bronze lions from Mentmore to Texas. He is an antiques shipper who has been trying to take the pain, suspense and financial guesswork out of importing antiques from England.'

Davis knows the power of glossy, professional publicity and has even produced his own newspaper, *Antiques Across the World*, the only free international newspaper for the antiques trade (see p. 58). Nor has his money-making expertise gone unnoticed: he was a 1978 winner of the Queen's Award for export and achievement. He is on record as saying that his aim is to become a total service company covering every aspect of the business, including accounts, travel, courier service (they have their own travel company), and more besides. 'We can quote, over the phone, a door-to-door rate for virtually anywhere in the world,' says Mr Davis. The company's computer logs all known specialist dealers by type and service in the UK and puts them on a mailing list. 'We point people in the right direction.' A further innovation is the instant telephone service in the UK: just ask the operator for Freephone 2304; it puts your call directly into Davis' sales quotation division. Even value added tax (the 'dealer's beast') is being defeated. 'We can't get VAT forms out of shippers is an old complaint,' says Mr Davis. 'Our computer punches out a customised letter with all the details.'

Because Davis has been for these past vital years intimately involved with the major movers of antiques across the Atlantic, he has been able to keep his fingers on the pulse of the market and capitalise on trends. The *New York Times* piece described a trip to his firm's warehouse as a perfect opportunity to see which way the fringe is blowing in the antique market. Even in 1977, Michael Davis was able to spot a 'definite trend to country pine'. He foresaw a penchant for Oriental pieces and a move towards polished steel. The *Times* writer remarked 'that an Arkansas dealer was building a collection of art nouveau; a Louisana dealer was stocking eighteenth- and nineteenth-century English; J. Robert Scott, the up-to-the-minute Los Angeles showroom, seemed to have cornered the market in chinoiserie vases, garden stalls and exotic bamboo occasional pieces; a Dallas dealer had a large collection of candlesticks and old steel milk cans ... and a New York antiques dealer was picking up apple baskets.' Not surprisingly, when Davis' New York office opened in 1979 it proved a resounding success. New York, he says, is now competing with London as the centre of the antiques market: 'We've completed a triangle. There are regular shipments back to London from New York; and New York trades with our West Coast office.' Being fully equipped to cater for trade to and from the USA Davis has not been slow to encourage UK dealers to exchange their pounds for dollars and sample the American atmosphere: in January 1980 he took a sizeable party of visitors across to the New York winter

antiques show; it enabled them to establish new contacts, build
a trading framework; it provided opportunities for newcomers,
and enabled buyers and sellers to exchange catalogues and
information.

When Michael Davis was old enough to go looking for a job,
he was no newcomer to retail trading on a massive scale: his
father owned Selmer, the foremost showroom for guitars and
brass strategically placed in the Charing Cross Road. When the
family removed to France, Davis went to work 'as a little clerk
in the purchasing department of Aristotle Onassis's Olympic
Maritime in Monaco'. There, he met his wife Carol. The couple
came back to England when Davis joined a deep-sea-diving
company, in their marketing division; his responsibility was
selling deep-sea-diving contracts for off-shore drilling installa-
tions. In the UK, Carol began work as a courier, driving foreign
buyers around to antique shops. At night, Davis would listen
to his wife's clients bemoaning the host of problems that then
besieged antique dealers. They cried about the slowness of
transport; the many breakages; currency problems; even down
to the sticky labels that left hideous and irremovable marks
when removed from furniture. Their moans were grist to the
marketing man's mill. By 1974, he had an office and bonded
warehouse in Los Angeles. To disentangle and rationalise
customs problems, he would discuss them with the customs
officers, often in person. Instead of laying down the law, his
opening gambit usually included the words, 'How do we do it;
how can we make life easier for you and at the same time for our
clients?'

Antique dealers are a classic example of business people who
have to be in two places at once — out on the road, buying, and
in the shop, selling. The fact that they are often in white-hot
competition with each other further aggravates the condition.
Davis knew he could offer dealers something valuable: more
time; time in which to buy antiques, rather than time wasted
digesting and processing official pieces of paper. His aim then
became the 'total care system'. So the company began to
organise travel, and accommodation, even down to reserving
theatre tickets. The company went further; it bought a town
house in London's Pimlico (a stone's throw from the King's
Road) and furnished it out in vividly coloured apartments; thus
there is a red flat, a beige flat, a green flat, a roof garden and
the possibility of booking by the week or less. Davis himself
lives near North Marlborough in Wiltshire; surrounding his own

seventeenth-century thatched house are a number of other properties, and these too have been turned into little havens of comfortable retreat for visiting antique dealers.

The real business of being in shipping, however, was business. It was not enough merely to point clients in the right direction; it made better sense to give them a detailed listing of the type of antique suppliers they wanted. Therefore Michael Davis circulated a questionnaire listing a rich variety of specialities so that dealers could tick off whichever applied to them, and the whole was fed into the recently acquired, and much vaunted, computer. Not only were overseas buyers then able to travel the length and breadth of the UK going right to the heart of their areas of interest, but they were able to do so handsomely kitted out with a folder containing specially prepared, non-marking, labels bearing the legend 'Michael Davis', which they affixed to their purchases, and then sat back to await delivery. No longer did buyers travelling under the auspices of Michael Davis even have to carry cash: it was left to the shippers to settle up with the various dealers after the purchasers had gone home.

When the purchase is made, the buyer simply gives the item a number, writes a number on the label and the number and price on a purchase order slip. At the end of the day this returns to Davis' company. A Davis truck then picks up the items (free in the London area) and pays for it. Here is where Michael Davis really scored: UK dealers used to wait three to four weeks for payment by shippers; the new regime turned that into an equivalent number of days.

The Davis success story has not been entirely without hiccups; at one time he actually went into the antiques business himself — and came a cropper, upsetting many rival dealers in the process. Apparently they baulked at the idea of having their own shipper as a potential competitor! Today Michael Davis is thrusting out in new and still more adventurous directions. In May 1980, he ferried a party of dealers to Hong Kong for the International Asian Antiques Fair. Their Hong Kong office opened in May 1979, and there is a representative office in Japan. Davis sees the Oriental scene opening up in a healthy way, and means to be there to capitalise on it. When Christie's held a major sale in Tokyo, it was Michael Davis who packed and cleared all the items. In August 1980, Davis capitalised on the focus of interest at the time of the Olympia Antiques Fair when he transported a party belonging to the

American Society of Interior Decorators (114 people) on a tour of the UK; they visited stately homes, stayed at the Gloucester Hotel, and probably did some buying at the same time.

The truth is, though, that the shipping antiques scene (containerloads of second-hand and often second-rate Edwardiana, Victorian wash-stands, hall-stands, and the bric-à-brac that used to clutter up the backyard of many a more tasteful dealer) is now on the wane. In 1977 Davis was sending out fifteen containers a week from Kew; now it is reduced to around twelve. His hope is to make further inroads into the fine art market, to break into the bastions of the longer-toothed art and antique dealers; to trade more with better quality and investment items. A further area for exploration has been the private moving business: as his advertising clearly trumpets: 'We've shipped for Lauren Bacall, Christopher Lee, Peter Schaffer, and several British peers, as well as an increasing number of diplomats taking up new posts.' And why not? If you can transport with care, and style, why not do it for those people whose own style can add verve to your own sales drive?

Danny Posner

In 1973 I wrote this about Danny Posner: 'By day Danny heads a busy and successful public relations firm. Out of hours he relaxes in his panelled "den", stacked from floor to ceiling with boys' books, story papers, dreadfuls, annuals, and much else besides. His aim is to get together a specimen copy of every kids' periodical ever published. Dreams like that cost money these days, and Danny has already invested thousands of pounds into his venture.'

Five years ago Danny opened the Vintage Magazine Shop in Earlham Street, London WC2. He had once also been a journalist, and the idea of purveying erstwhile popular journalism was a congenial one. His hobbyist's dream, however, was not to remain parochial. Today Danny's stock is valued at upwards of £2½ million; he runs a similar shop in San Francisco, and others are planned for New York and Manchester. The success of the operation has been overwhelming; of an estimated 5,000 customers a week, 1,000 put their hands in their pocket and buy. Because of the busy location in Brewer Street, Soho, many customers (as many as 20 per cent, Posner estimates) are first-time buyers. The London shop alone employs eight people, as well as two part-timers.

How did he make the transition from PR executive to full-time professional dealer? In a way, it was success at his other entrepreneurial work that drove him to it. 'I was publicist for the rock group Emerson, Lake and Palmer, running all over the world; people kept approaching me — would I manage them, too. I didn't mind the idea of being the new Brian Epstein, but then I discovered that all the effort was going out from me, but no money was coming in.' Then a musician in one of his fledgeling groups, who was running a stall in Earlham Street in the West End of London, heard that the shop just behind his pitch was about to require a new tenant.

'I thought it would be a marvellous second string business, in addition to being a rock "magician",' says Posner. Then the musician lost interest. Danny had a choice: go it alone or abandon the venture. 'I stuck some of my own collection in the shop, and sat back.' That metaphorical posture is not particularly apt, for he was swept off his feet in the rush to see, to sell, and to buy. As he says, 'From the response I was getting, and from reports, I realised that mine was the only shop of its type in the world.'

The Vintage Magazine Shop was born in January 1975. Being in the heart of London's West End there was an abundance of passing trade — but also furiously high overheads. Clearly Danny could not charge junk shop prices of 10p a comic; there was no future in that. Nor was he, however, in a market place where there were accepted, and economically acceptable, price levels, a received status structure for comic collectables; he had *established* the market place. It was up to him to make it financially viable. His success would depend, among other things, on his ability to judge correctly the prices people would be prepared to pay. Among those who thought his venture was scheduled for a swift nosedive were his friends and fellow comic buffs, the members of the Old Boys' Book Club; they gave him six months. Once he had sold off his own collection, they thought he would be through. In the event, they suffered from the insular 'tunnel vision' that has afflicted many finger-wagging and pusillanimous collectors. Collectors, who are so often extremely knowledgeable about their subjects, can sometimes think they know it all in other areas, too. The comic and story paper collectors were convinced that they knew the extent of the market — Danny estimates that the universe of serious comic collectors consisted of no more than three to four hundred people at that time. That was merely the current *au fait* market; the potential market had yet to be realised.

In a way the clique had controlled the market. Anyone who was dealing was doing it out of his own home; prices were kept artificially low to stop them escalating. Selling to each other in a protectionist way has an endearing charm, and is about as friendly as collecting ever gets. Nevertheless, it was an artificial state of affairs. 'I had to be prepared to pay more to buy stock, and also to stop the people who were still throwing magazines away. People wouldn't throw books away, but they would discard magazines; they were ephemeral, not worth keeping. I had to convince them that they were.' Danny travelled to Birmingham to pay £1,500 to a man who had collected bundles of magazines which had been left on pavements for the dustmen. 'Once people knew I was paying out-of-the-world prices, they started bringing magazines in.'

One simple expedient was to price everything at £1 or more. Even at the new inflated rate people were, says Danny, looking in the window and 'going ga-ga' at the prospect. They also came in to buy. It was not only the lure of nostalgia, he insists; people who were born far later than the classic comics, like *Magnet, Gem, Rover, Wizard* and *Hotspur,* were fascinated by the 'lure of times gone'.

Initially Danny stuck to his own period: nothing later than 1945. Then, it became clear that the demand was there for 1950s and 1960s publications. It was not confined to English periodicals, either; French and American magazines were also in big demand. Danny reasoned that if there was an enthusiastic following for American magazines in this country, there might also be a market for English 'rubbish' in the USA.

Because Vintage Magazines was already tapping a lucrative market in movie ephemera (movie buffs would travel out from Hollywood on a buying expedition and would never waste a journey, he says) Danny was all but convinced that the West Coast was the place to be. Film aficionados are hungry for old movie stills, movie posters (which the shop also stocks), cinema trade papers; general magazines are also often bought just for their movie content. When Ken Russell was researching his film *Valentino* he spent several days in the shop poring over old photographs of the heart-throb star of the 1920s — just to see how earlier lensmen had deployed their lights. The professional marketing man in Posner, however, had to be sure that the location was right and that the American market was as strong as he suspected it was. Fortunately one of his colleagues working in London at that time lived in San Francisco and he was able to go to the West Coast and spend seven weeks researching the market. Only then, in the summer of 1979, did he establish himself in the USA, with his son Frank managing the shop.

Danny spent the early days of the London shop buying stock; he was terrified that he might run out of things to sell. Dealing and collecting are not always the easiest of bedfellows; it is so tempting to keep the best for oneself. Nevertheless, as prime specimens flooded into the shop he began to get blasé; he would take home volumes, enjoy them, then put them back in to sell. His aim now is to establish a 'shop collection' — a permanent, inviolable display. In the event, his furious buying exercise he now recognises as having been the basis for his later success. His first year was a struggle; in the second year business took a 50 per cent upturn; and in the third year he was away. The market began to expand, to develop in ways that could not have been envisaged. The shop began as a collector's treasure house; but there is a whole service industry locked up in old ephemera, apparently, and Danny has begun to tap it profitably. Television, film and theatrical companies are regular customers; they need period publications as props, to give an authentic look to a stage or set. They also are guided by the clothes people used to wear in old magazines. A jeans company was building an advertising campaign around an historic theme — jeans had been popular in the UK since the 1950s, but they had been standard working men's garb in the USA a hundred years earlier. The firm turned to picture papers to see exactly how the British wore their jeans thirty years ago. A nationally known baking group, when they were researching one of their nostalgic advertisements, also made use of the vast storehouse of reference material in the shop. In the advertisement, two schoolboys watch the Flying Scotsman thunder by. The company needed to know what the boys might have had in their satchels, how the interior of the driver's cab might have looked, and so on. The comics helped. The *Sunday Times* magazine carried an article on the greatest Meccano collector in the world and looked to Danny's pile of old Meccano magazines for additional reference material. A Canadian barber who wanted to call his new salon Sweeney Todd delved into the comic archives, right back to the Penny Dreadfuls of the

An issue of Union Jack, *price 2d, dated 11 August 1928. This boy's thriller is from the collection of Danny Posner. Posner, for years a collector of vintage magazines, is now head of a business selling old magazines and ephemera with shops in the USA and London.*

Victorian years, in search of attractive decoration for his walls.

As a rule, though, Danny will not sell comics as decorative prints; he despises those who tear off the colour covers (notably those by famed illustrators such as Erté or Vargas), frame them, and sell them as original prints. Nor is he keen to sell to museums or libraries. 'Comics should be handled, enjoyed — even if it does mean that they fall apart.' There seems to be no easy way to preserve the cheaper type of comic; made, as they were of cheap stock, they will surely turn to dust; this is, perhaps, one of the charms of ephemera.

In 1973, when first we spoke, Danny revealed that some clairvoyant collectors were laying down series of papers, as if they were fine wine. Almost every 'run' (several consecutive issues, or a complete year of publication) is sure to accrue in value, he said. The same still applies. He tips today's *Vogue* magazine, and 'rock' papers, like *Melody Maker* and *New Musical Express* and the current movie magazines, as the money-spinning ephemera for years to come. As for the *crème de la crème* early magazines, a No. 1 *Beano* is currently fetching £50 to £100, depending on condition.

Children's comics, like toys, were never meant to last, and any that have escaped the ravages of time, sticky probing fingers and the paint pot (children's books so often carry quaint little nursery doodles that are harmless fun but cut the value dramatically) are bound to sell for a premium. Because Danny felt that the demand for early issues was out of step with the poor supply of originals, he contacted D.C. Thomson, the supposedly intractable publishers of 'the big five' (*Adventure, Rover, Wizard, Skipper* and *Hotspur*) as well as *Beano*. Could he reprint their immortal early issues at his own expense? The publishers agreed, with one stipulation: that the issues be bound together in book form, presumably to prevent comic-size facsimiles being palmed off as pristine originals by unscrupulous punters. Thus was D.C. Thomson Firsts born, and it is still selling like the proverbial hot cakes. Danny claims that there are thousands more bundles of old comics in attics: atrophy of the source of supply is not one of his nightmares any more. He sees new possibilities round every frontier. *Eagle*, for instance, one of the best-loved large format papers, with space traveller Dan Dare and the green-tinged egg-head alien, the Mekon, was a great success in the UK, but the comic was never issued in the USA. Surely, with a little encouragement, the Americans will also be fascinated by it, he reasons.

Then there are collectors from the Continent and even further afield. A shop in every capital is hardly practicable, but comics are the ideal mail order collectable. With hundreds of enquiry letters coming in every week, the interest looked strong enough. Shrewdly, Posner did not attempt to set up his own mailing department, or hurriedly try to 'educate' himself in the intricacies of mail order — not when time away from his mainstream, over-the-counter operation meant money lost. He took over a competitor, someone in a similar line of business, in a small way, who agreed to manage his postal section. Currently there are 10,000 firm orders on file; people who are waiting for the right picture, right issue or run of a magazine to come in.

[7]
Advice on Setting up Your Business

Trade organisations

In the UK, the three main trade organisations for dealers are
BADA (British Antique Dealers' Association), LAPADA
(London and Provincial Antique Dealers' Association) and
SLAD (Society of London Art Dealers). The prime function of a
trade association is to further the interests of its members.
Nonetheless, these three non-profit-making bodies set out to be
rather more than a freemasonry of dealers. Antique and art
dealers do not always get a good Press. Though they are the
exception, not the rule, stories of old ladies parting with
valuable heirlooms for a few pounds to a smooth-talking
knocker make good newspaper articles. In the popular imagination a knocker is merely a rogue dealer, an opinion that is often
confirmed when, as often happens, the law is powerless to bring
about redress. Court reports in which the defendant accused of
dishonestly handling goods describes himself as 'an antique
dealer' do not help either. The associations are not, however,
PR set-ups designed to do a facelift on a shifty image. Members
are required to be knowledgeable, experienced (usually three
years in the trade), vouched for by established members or
dealers who have spent many years in the trade, to be VAT
registered, and to have a fixed place of business open to the
public. LAPADA members enjoy other benefits, such as
assistance with legal and tax problems, authentication of
antiques for export, specialist Lloyds insurance cover, comprehensive packing and shipping service, BUPA medical
insurance, discounts on insurance, cars and van hire, hotels,
certain publications, information on stolen goods, a classified
directory of members, a regular newsletter, publicity to
overseas buyers and display aids. It also helps members in
dispute with the public over a purchase. (See p. 143.)

Business name registration

The name you give your antique business can spell out your particular line or attract by the way it rolls off the tongue. London boasts Just Desks, China Choice, Cameo Corner, Pleasures of Past Times, Antiquus, Anno Domini and the intriguingly named Antique Pussy. Essex has Bits and Pieces, Trade Wind, Tempus Fugit; there's the Chair Shop in Oxted, the Brass Skillet in Dorset, and Circa 1800 in Edinhurgh.

Remember that it is necessary to register a business name (unless you trade under your unadorned own name) with the Registry of Business Names, Companies House, 55–71 City Road, London EC1Y 1BB, before you begin trading. It has been estimated that only some 5 per cent of those who ought to register actually bother, and there are efforts being made to scrap the requirement. Nevertheless it is still a legal obligation in the UK.

Insurance

Insurance is so important in the art and antiques world that Sotheby's set up Artscope International Insurance Services in 1979 to provide insurance for private, commercial and institutional owners of works of art. The household names in insurance are helpful and knowledgeable when it comes to insuring household things; they are often wooden and blank where fine art is concerned. A good broker may help, or the information service at Lloyds.

Security

Three hundred thousand homes are burgled annually in the UK. Portsmouth Crime Prevention Panel offers the following tips on security. Photograph all your more valuable portable items, including small furniture and longcase clocks. To indicate size, place a ruler alongside. Colour photographs are preferable for porcelain and pictures.

Silverware
Make a note or sketch of identifiable features, e.g. initials, family crests, and any damage such as a dent or repair.

Hallmarks are also important — free literature is available from the Assay Offices and inexpensive booklets from most booksellers. A study of these will help identify and date your silver.

Clocks and watches
Make a note of the maker, the type of face and numerals, the material and decoration of the case. The back of a clock may bear old repair marks scratched into the metal.

Medals and jewellery
Note the title of each decoration and record any inscriptions and names. Try and identify stones and settings in jewellery. Your jeweller may help — again a photograph is best.

Values
Make a full list of your valuables and get them properly valued nd insured.

Photography

An antique dealer will want to be able to use a camera and to own one that is good enough for the purpose in hand. A lot of dealing is done by sending colour or black and white snaps through the post. They will not win any photographic competitions but the detail is usually sufficiently clear for most purposes. When trying to indicate size remember to include something of known dimensions alongside, like a matchbox, stamp, coin, or pack of cigarettes.

Auction houses prefer black and white pictures when identifying items; they find that colours are so often inaccurate, especially with amateur photographs and prints (as opposed to transparencies) that they can mislead.

Many people use single lens reflex cameras. These are very versatile and can be used with a wide range of lenses, including close-up lenses and wide angle lenses which can take in a near panoramic scene from quite close to (though beware the distortion that sometimes occurs at the corners with very wide angle lenses). The 35 mm film used, however, is quite small and will need to be enlarged. If you use a larger format camera, the contact prints alone are often clear enough to serve as reference shots.

Fire protection

Anyone setting up shop should take expert advice on fire protection from the outset. Help is available, free, in the UK, from your local fire prevention officer who is based at fire brigade area headquarters. The Fire Protection Association, at Aldermary House, Queen Street, London EC4, issues data sheets on fire safety and also gives relevant information in its bi-monthly journal *Fire Prevention.* Legal requirements are set out in the Guide to Fire Precautions 1971 Act No. 3: Offices, Shops and Railway Premises, issued by the Home Office and available from HMSO. Some simple measures include the following. Avoid inflammable interior finishes and highly combustible furniture of the foam rubber type. Where possible deter smokers. Investigate the cost of installing a heat detector which can trigger an alarm. Sprinkler systems are extremely effective but it is not unknown for water and smoke to do more damage than fire itself. A gas flooding system may be an alternative: carbon dioxide or another inert gas smothers the flames without damaging goods.

It may be possible for certain fabrics to be treated so as to be flame-retardant. Asbestos curtains or curtaining made of woven glass fibre and fire doors can help contain fires. Keep extinguishers handy and make sure that your staff know how to call the fire brigade and can operate fire prevention devices.

Be sure that electric points are not overloaded and that all equipment is turned off, preferably at the mains, at the end of the day. Spotlights are notoriously badly designed and frequently overheat around the lamp, so burning away the protective covering of the flex. Check periodically that wiring is in good condition.

Outside windows should be well protected with shutters, as a precaution against arson. If you have a yard and store goods in it, be sure that they are well away from the stray matches and cigarette butts that are carelessly discarded over walls.

[8]
Future Trends

Fashions change with the times and this is as true for antiques as for other fields of interest and acquisition. Yet it is possible to attempt to predict trends for the future.

In the increasingly fraught world of the antique trader it is perhaps understandable that he does not always enjoy a reputation as the cheeriest retailer in the high street. Private customers can sometimes be made to feel downright unwelcome as the trade buyer with the overstuffed wallet darts about buying without hesitation. 'Trade Only' signs in shop windows only serve to hammer home the message. If traders are truly worried that auction rooms are winning the battle for customers then they will have to take positive steps to win back lost business. This might include opening at regular times, or, if this is impractical and must be limited to one or two days a week or weekends, making sure that the hours are prominently displayed and adhered to.

Selling to a dealer should not be a hazardous proposition. It is up to the trade to spell out the advantages and ostracise those who flaunt the unwritten rules of fair play. A dealer can pay cash on the nail, unlike an auction house which may take weeks to pay and will then deduct perhaps 20 per cent in commission and expenses. If a dealer can offer a buy-back policy (at the purchase price, at any time) that too will inspire confidence. A customer who feels he has been unfairly treated will not return, and may even be the cause of unwelcome publicity.

In Sweden auctions are being televised and bids taken over the telephone. In the USA the 'tag' sale is catching on with home owners who want to sell their treasures *in situ*. House sales are traditionally better attended and more successful than salerooms: furniture and paintings look more enticing in their proper setting. An auction house representative prices the items according to the latest saleroom figures, and affixes price tags. The sale is advertised locally by the owner of the house.

The saleroom collects the money, deducting its commission (about 25 per cent), but the buyer pays no premium. Sotheby's are said to be showing an interest in getting involved in tag sales, which is not good news for many antique dealers.

Pacemakers to watch

Everybody can be a pundit, in antiques as in any other sphere; I prefer to listen to those who 'put their money where their mouth is'. However, successful business people did not reach their present position by turning commercial secrets into public statements. *Faute de mieux,* we have to turn to the informed, dispassionate observers of the market and the sorting houses of the antiques world — the auction rooms.

Phillips' *Antiques at Auction Survey, 1979–80* included the following as pacemakers to watch in 1980: late Victorian and Edwardian furniture; oak reproduction 1860–1920; tea caddies; treen; quality Victorian paintings; eighteenth-century mezzo-tints; English nineteenth-century bracket clocks; good scientific instruments; nineteenth-century electrical equipment; caucasian, Hamadan, Malayer and Shiraz carpets; English Delft tiles; signed Royal Worcester; George II silver; old Sheffield plate; art pottery by Leach, Cardew, Vyse; automobilia; sporting memorabilia; Russian and Chinese bonds; photographs.

In 1978 Robin Duthy, a freelance investment consultant, wrote a book called *Alternative Investment* (Michael Joseph). He investigated ten areas: books, Chinese ceramics, coins, diamonds, English silver, firearms, gold, modern prints, stamps and French wine. In each field he compiled a hypothetical portfolio of objects and monitored the performance of representative examples of their class from 1950 to time of writing. It is clear that it has been possible to make spectacular gains in certain areas at a time when traditional investment, like the Stock Exchange, were absymal performers.

Another weighty addition to the literature available to the serious investor is the report published by The Economist Intelligence Unit Ltd, entitled *Art As Investment*. This included fourteen different art categories in painting, prints, books, ceramics, glass, silver and furniture. The method used was to take as samples objects sold at major auctions in the UK or USA at least twice between 1960 and 1979. A work by the artist Magritte bought in 1961 and sold in 1979 showed an increase in value of 4,652 per cent, which was 4,370 per cent better than an average investment on Wall Street over the same period. Dealers in the higher echelons of the market (and private investors) will benefit most from such high powered material. Nevertheless, the general lesson is clear: quality goods appreciate at the highest rate; always buy the best you can afford.

Collectable crafts

Furniture and furnishings from the arts and crafts movement of the early years of this century are much in demand today. Tomorrow it might be the crafts of our own leading exponents. Look at the illustrated guide *Craftsmen of Quality* issued by the Crafts Advisory Committee (12 Waterloo Place, London SW1Y 4AU). It is a pictorial guide to the work of masters in the arts of glass blowing, painting, etching and engraving, leatherwork, metalwork, textiles, toys and puppets, and more. John Makepeace has already been acclaimed as 'England's best known craft furniture maker'. The cover of *Furniture, A Concise History*, by Edward Lucie Smith, from whom the quotation comes, shows a chair by Makepeace. The carver, of stunning elegance, seems to combine, in its high backed elegance, the work of Rennie Mackintosh, Thonet (for its smooth curves), Chippendale Gothic (for the pointed back), and the lightness of *bergere* canework in the seat and back. Makepeace works from Parnham, a superb seventeenth-century mansion near Beaminster in Dorset where he also trains promising young craftsmen. 'Parnham in London' was a well received exhibition of the work of the master and his protegés put on at the British Crafts Centre in 1979.

The work of fabric sculptor Felicity Youett, who studied painting at the Royal College of Art, may also qualify as a future hedge against inflation. Youett has taken her inspiration from the hard, angular structures and the detritus of urban life and transformed these images into soft, padded satin sculptures. Thus a wall and door is hung with shimmering satin petals perfectly shaped to look like the ivy leaves that inspired them. Torn hoardings led to a tassled satin eiderdown; spilling rubbish in a factory yard prompted a striking three-dimensional patchwork design for cushion covers. Skyscrapers feature in a wall hanging of sewn and stuffed satin. Set against a wall sprayed to look like sky they offered a chic backdrop to a town-house dining area with no view of its own.

Victorian and Edwardian reproduction furniture in imitation of Sheraton, Chippendale and Hepplewhite is already collected for its own merits. Even these 'respectable' reproductions, however, are not available in sufficient quantity to satisfy the demand, and business is booming for furniture-makers who can recreate the furniture of the age of elegance. William Tillman of London SW1 makes Sheraton-style breakfast tables for £1,146; the eighteenth-century style walnut cabinet of Arthur Brett & Sons of Norwich is currently priced at over £10,000. Yet still this is cheaper than a period original — assuming that you can find one. There is a fair chance that furniture of this quality and exclusivity will gain in value as the price of skilled labour soars and the years go by, adding their own layers of patina to confuse further the issue of what is real and what is reproduction.

Art in business

Mr Wengraf of Colnaghi's gallery (owned by Jacob Rothschild) believes that businessmen will not invest in art unless they can see the point aesthetically. 'If a businessman lacks that taste, if he can't tell the difference between leather and leatherette, he won't pay out £20,000 for wall decoration.' Jim Slater, once the brightest star in the City, could see the point, and by 1970 had cornered much of the world market in paintings by a then relatively unknown Victorian landscape painter, Frederick William Watts, In the late 1960s Slater's personal hoard of Watts pictures had gone up fourfold in value, from £25,000 to £100,000. When the crash came he was forced to sell some pictures at a considerable loss, but the strategy had been sound.

Firms are coming to appreciate that carefully bought fine furniture, paintings or porcelain not only improve in value, but they are also delightful to look at. And what better place to enjoy that beauty than in the crucible of power — the boardroom. Booker McConnell, owners of Budgen Supermarkets, Lemon Hart Rum and Tia Maria were the biggest British company in Guyana and ran the sugar industry. They had been in the country since 1815 and their boardroom was festooned with views of the company's holdings painted in 1821 by J. Bryant when they came up for auction in

Amsterdam; and it soon proved a worthwhile investment. The evidence suggests that shareholders feel better about their company investing in art if there is some obvious historical connection.

Magazines

Almost every run (unbroken series) of a magazine acquires value. Danny Posner, owner of Vintage Magazines (see Chapter 6), recommends laying down *Vogue* magazines (a book celebrating *Vogue* covers from 1909 to 1940 appeared in 1980). The illustrious casualties of commercial journalism must also qualify as collectables. *Nova,* a much admired chronicle of the trend setter, ran for several years before foundering. The Titanic of magazines, in terms of cash and kudos lost, was probably the *Mirror* magazine. *Value Today* was a brave effort that crashed after only a couple of issues. In 1972 an American company, extensively involved in popular music, decided to buy *B.M.G.* (Banjo, Mandolin and Guitar) magazine, a monthly magazine founded in 1903, and update its faded image. The experiment yielded a handful of issues, the covers of which show a sequence of change in style and presentation quite unparalleled in the history of journalism. When the Americans lost interest it was sold back to its British owners who promptly returned it to its anachronistic, but economically viable, splendour. Collections that tell a story, even a sad one, are often good news eventually — for collectors.

The relics of rock music

The hardware of 'Rock 'n' Roll', the juke boxes that frequently turn up at auction and are knocked down for over a thousand pounds, and the guitars which can also go for four figures (like those made by the American firms of Martin, Gibson and Fender), are as out of reach as Chinese Chippendale to most people. I do know, however, of one guitarist who has sunk his money into a roomful of Martin folk guitars, all of which, the taxman agrees, he needs to own, to play and perform. He bought most of them cheaply and is now comfortable in the knowledge that several are worth the price of a cottage in the country.

No, it is the ephemera of rock, still available in trunkloads, that is awaiting thorough exploitation by buyers on a budget. Take Elvis Presley, for example. Since his death, this rock star has become very collectable. Before the 'King' signed with RCA, he made five single records which now turn around on the market for something close to £200. And the sleeves, so often thrown away, are worth even more.

At Antiquarius, in London's King's Road, there is a stand selling Beatles and Rolling Stones magazines and *The Beatles Monthly,* a fan club publication which ran for seven years. There must be plenty of those about — worth finding at £1 a copy resale price. The Beatles spawned a whole trinket industry, with guitar shaped pins, brooches, drink coasters, diaries (each £5), tablecloths (£10), handkerchiefs (£3), tin trays (£10), Corgi tin model yellow submarines (£30). Most coveted of all Beatle items is an American LP record cover show-

Early Beatle 'giveaways', because they were often also thrown away, are desired by the rockiana collector. This early Beatles poster, in luminous green, red and blue, came free with a teenage magazine.

ing the four lads dressed as butchers' packing dolls. It was too
bloody for the authorities, who banned it. Now the cover alone
goes for £100.

The plastic age

As much as there was a bronze and an iron age, our own may go
down in history as the plastic age. So it would seem smart to
collect plastic artefacts for our sons and daughters. Unfortun-
ately, however, they are already being collected, and in quite
some style. The Victoria and Albert Museum lays down objects
for future generations of students and included plastic in its
exhibition 'Objects the V&A Collects' in the late 1970s. The
'Synthetic Jewellery and Gems' exhibition at the Goldsmiths'
Hall in 1979 also showed a fascination for man-made materials,
including jewellery from the 1920s and 1930s.

Plastic has a more venerable history than you may think.
Alexander Parkes, a Birmingham inventor, patented a plastic
in 1855, a fact celebrated by British Industrial Plastics Ltd
who set up a touring display of plastic products from the 1850s
to the 1950s. What can you hope to buy? I have an orange
squeezer, with detachable drip tray in lurid mottled yellow and
orange plastic, 'a "DODCA" product'. Fountain pens in
mottled or tortoiseshell plastic, like the old Conway Stewarts,
are worth buying. Jewellery, sometimes brightened up with
chrome plate, is fun to find. Some of the best jewellery was
made by Paco Rabanne (of male cologne fame) in the 1960s.
Plastic was used to imitate tortoiseshell, jet, ivory or amber.
The best items are unashamedly plastic without the masque-
rade. Centrepiece of a plastic collection might be an example of
designer Charles Eames's DAR chair of 1948 in glass-fibre
reinforced plastic.

Giveaways

Advertising memorabilia is a well established collector's
province. Modern advertising will doubtless one day become
desirable, too. The *Sunday Times Magazine* showed a collection
of manufacturers' knick-knacks, either giveaways (plastic
ephemera?) or available cut-price. Such things as the Homepride flour shaker, in the form of a little man in a bowler hat,

and the blow-up Michelin tyre man were featured. The Homepride man is usually black and white, but a silver version came out in Jubilee year.

Many commemoratives were struck for Queen Elizabeth II's Jubilee in 1977. Barrie Quinn [of Barrie Quinn Antiques, London] commissioned this special commemorative jardinière, hand finished in silver leaf, in a limited edition of 500, each signed and numbered. The jardinière would probably now sell at almost double its original price.

Limited editions

I was once intrigued to discover that a shirt I had bought, made by Mr Harry (latterly Rael-Brook), had a label informing me that it was a limited edition. Perhaps I should have sealed it in plastic and propped it up in my display case along with the mug commemorating the landing of man on the moon in July 1969, the pincushion ladies and the Moorcroft pots. I wore it out instead. Soon after, a firm advertised a limited edition of paintings on glass, with the name Constable boldly featured. They were signed on the back, the advertisement said. By Constable exhumed? No, by the company's glass artist who did not rate a mention in the sales blurb. Nor, indeed, did the number to which the paintings were to be limited. For they were to be limited by date. So if half a million people wrote in and ordered before the closing date, and stocks held up, the limited number could have been 500,000. Some cachet!

That is the trouble with limited editions. You have to read the small print and be psychic into the bargain, to know which of the gilded porcelain plates, pewter chessmen and wild life plaques are going to soar in value. If in doubt about buying, telephone an auction house in London for their verdict on limited editions. Most are a flop at auction, they will say; there must be something 'phoney' about contriving rarity these days in manufactured items, There have been successes, however, notably some porcelain figures of Queen Elizabeth II on horseback. Even items commemorating recent events are worth considering, as they were limited by event (i.e. mostly lost or discarded after the show), if not by number, they are cheap to buy, and are unlikely to be faked for some time yet.

One of the great Jubilee jokes was the commemorative chamber pot made by Portmeirion pottery in Stoke; but the Lord Chamberlain, on behalf of the Queen, was not amused, So the potters added a second handle. As a result, Her Majesty was pleased to accept her new 'planter' — No. 1 in a limited edition of 500.

Illustrators' art

I have to declare an interest in illustrators' art, as I deal in it. There is a growing awareness of the quality of the work of contemporary illustrators whose work appears in the Press, in advertising, on television, record sleeves and so on. There are currently about five galleries selling illustrators' work in London. The aim must be to own a classic piece of advertising or famous record sleeve and the original artwork from which the illustration was taken. Book illustrations are already collectable as fine art. Today's collector should respond, too, to magazine illustrators. Leading exponents are Michael Trevithick, Bob Lawrie, Lars Hokanson, Tony Wright, Mick Brownfield, Celestino Valenti, Peter Brookes, Brian Grimwood and Bush Hollyhead. Richard Kennedy's illustrations for children's books and book jackets are already minor classics. Original drawings from his limited edition books published by the Whittington Press (*The Song of Songs* and *Garden of the Night*) must prove worthwhile investments in the long term.

(9)
Running a Stand in an Antiques Fair

In 1974 I met Felicity Simmonds who, with her late husband, had just begun Step-in Markets. In the *Daily Mail's* 'Money Mail' section I wrote: 'Cash from antiques, an old story, has been given a Cinderella twist. Collectors now have the opportunity to become dealers for a day.

'If you're a collector with an oversize collection it means you can sell off "doubles", or pieces you've fallen out of love with — and you don't have to set up shop to do it.'

It sounds an easy introduction to the antique market and it is; it is also cheap. Knowing some of the pitfalls, however, can help turn even your very first time out into a profit-making venture. The first rule is to be prepared. Leave nothing until the last minute, because business starts, usually, from about 9 am, with the trade being admitted first to the hall that has been hired for the event. Fairs are often held at the weekend, and the dealers like to visit all of the weekend antique markets as well as the fairs. Some will not arrive till late in the day, having placed your market last in their itinerary, but some will burst in when it opens, and they will be in a hurry. Make sure everything is priced, or at least that its price is in your head; nothing is so offputting and worrying to a potential purchaser as a stallholder who does not know how much he wants for an item. Little sticky labels are fine for some articles, but if they leave a trace of glue they can be unsuitable for glass or delicate porcelain. Also get a supply of tie-on labels for knick-knacks like jewellery, hatpins, and so on.

You will probably have a long rectangular table. Have you got a long enough table cloth? A display with half a cloth does not look impressive. Dark velvet or felt is very good; do not use anything vigorously patterned as you will 'lose' some of your little antiques in the intricacies of the design!

You will need to take with you the following: scissors, Scotch tape, string, wrapping paper (for take-homes and for sales), a receipt book and a piece of carbon paper so that you have a replica of the receipts for your own records, and a hamper of food to sustain you through the day. Some fairs last from early in the morning until 5 pm, so hot soup, sandwiches and fruit are a good idea. Also take a friend. You will need him or her when you get bored stiff with nothing happening or when you are run off your feet with customers and unable to keep an eye on what they are all doing. If you must go alone, a neighbouring dealer will almost always look after your pitch as a returnable favour, but you must expect to be neglected (and perhaps lose a sale) if he is called away to serve one of his own clients.

As someone may have to take money for you, this is another reason to have everything clearly marked. It is taken as read that a pound or two here is an allowable discount from about £9 and upwards, with 10 per cent acceptable over this figure to many traders. The little inset in some price tags, 'T4' for example, may mean that trade can have £4 off a £38 article, but it is one of those codes that is meant to be broken; a private customer claims what he takes to be the trade discount and will often not try to beat down further, although he would succeed if he persevered.

Stands are usually distributed in a large rectangular hall, some in the centre, forming a rectangle parallel with the walls; other stands will go around the walls. Which should you choose? The wall stands are often dearer, not only because you can prop things up against the wall, rest shelving against it etc, but you are much more likely to have the use of electric points in the wall, which means you can take portable spotlights to brighten up your show. People coming through a door are more likely to circulate clockwise, turning first to the left. On the assumption that visitors spend as they go, you may be able to take tactical advantage of this curious fact. Being near the door is an obvious advantage.

In any market place, even in one as relatively genteel as an antiques market, there is a need to attract attention. Contrary to popular belief, antiques do *not* sell themselves; they need to be sold. This is a two-stage operation. They must first be well displayed. Your table is flat so it is a good idea to bring with you a miniature whatnot, small bookshelves, even an orange box or washing-up rack (the tall sort) covered with cloth, to create vertical planes — anything to catch the eye, and enable you to present more per square foot of table space. If you have small, valuable trinkets you will want safety pins to attach them, safely, to baize or silk. Very pricey things will need to go under glass, with the opening of the case turned towards you, not the customer. 'Rubbish' of all sorts sells. Even if you have fine bronze or porcelain it is a good idea to have the equivalent of the supermarket's lossleader, for example a pile of junk for pence. One dealer has 50p items with a placard that reads 'Nothing over £1000'. If you have a very good day you will need to replenish stock; your reserve stock can be kept under the table, suitably covered up with newspaper to thwart sticky fingers.

Every so often you will want to stretch your legs (another reason for working with a partner). Do not go out, go round the hall. See what other dealers are up to. Chat to them; watch what sells and how they do it. Some traders take very little money on a particular fair, but they reckon their time well spent if they do some good buying. Perhaps the most important lesson to learn is that people need to be coaxed into a sale. Of course the professional with little time on his hands and a fat roll of notes in his pocket will act smartly, but you will need to chat to private customers as often as not.

Ask if they collect whatever is holding their interest. Tell them some interesting fact about the item. Suggest that you can 'help' them with the price. All of the rules of salesmanship apply to antiques: you must create a special relationship with your client, as often as not, before you can clinch a sale.

Try to carry a range of goods (books, pictures, pots, glasses), then you will always have somebody looking round your stall; remember how people flock to the market stall when someone is holding forth about a patent potato peeler; people attract people Another trick of the trade is to rearrange your stock from time to time, adding a bit of your reserve to vary the scene. The same buyers sometimes circulate for hours and will stop if they see that something new has appeared. Some will also come back later in the day in the hope that you will drop your price dramatically in the final minutes in order to boost your day's takings and save taking an item home again.

If you are offered a cheque always ask to see not only a cheque guarantee card (take down the details on the back of the cheque) but also some other form of identification such as a driving licence. (This may also have been stolen, of course, but you would eliminate the crook who has stolen just a cheque book and card.) If the amount is greater than the cheque card figure you can ask for several cheques to make up the total, or say you will have to clear the cheque first; give a receipt and perhaps even offer to deliver the goods yourself. Dealers expect to be 'knocked' from time to time, but it remains true that there are more honest people about than dishonest.

Appendix

Addresses of Relevant Organisations in the UK

Trade Organisations

BADA, 20 Rutland Gate, London SW7 1BD
LAPADA, 112 Brompton Road, London SW3 1JJ
SLAD, 41 Norfolk Avenue, Sanderstead,
South Croydon CR2 8BT

Clubs and societies

Antique Collectors' Club, 5 Church Street, Woodbridge, Suffolk
The Ephemera Society, 12 Fitzroy Square, London W1
The International Correspondence of Corkscrew Addicts,
Warren Rowe, 25 St Edmund's Avenue, Ruislip, Middlesex
City of London Phonograph and Gramophone Society, John
McKeown, Eccentric Club, 9 Ryde Street, St James's,
London SW1Y 6PZ

Select list of auctioneers and salerooms

London
Bonhams, W. & F.C. Bonham & Sons Ltd, Montpelier
Galleries, Montpelier Street, London SW7 1HH (Tel:
01-584 9161/589 4577; Tgms: Bonhams London SW7; Telex:
916477 Bonham G)
Bonhams, New Chelsea Galleries, 65-69 Lots Road, London
SW10 (Tel: 01-352 0466)
Christie, Manson & Woods Ltd, 8 King Street, St James's,
London SW1Y 6QT (Tel: 01-839 9060; Tgms: Christiart
London SW1; Telex: 916429)
Christie's South Kensington, 85 Old Brompton Road, London

SW7 3JS (Tel: 01-581 2231; Telex: 916429)

Glendining & Co, Blenstock House, 7 Blenheim Street, New Bond Street, London W1Y 0AS (Tel: 01-493 2445/6/7; Telex: 298855)

Harrods Auction Galleries, Arundel Terrace, Barnes, London SW13 9DT (Tel: 01-748 2739)

Phillips, Blenstock House, 7 Blenheim Street, New Bond Street, London W1Y 0AS (Tel: 01-629 6602; Tgms: Auctions London W1; Telex: 298855 Blen G)

Phillips West 2, Salem Road, London W2 (Tel: 01-221 5303)

Phillips Marylebone, The Marylebone Auction Rooms, Hayes Place, Lisson Grove, London NW1 (Tel: 01-723 2647)

Sotheby Parke Bernet & Co, 34 & 35 New Bond Street, London W1A 2AA (Tel: 01-493 8080; Tgms: Abinitio; Telex: 24454)

Hodgson's Rooms (Sotheby Parke Bernet & Co), 115 Chancery Lane, London WC2A 1PX (Tel: 01-405 7238; Tgms: Bookhood London WC2; Telex: 24454)

Sotheby's Belgravia, 19 Motcomb Street, London SW1X 8LB (Tel: 01-235 4311; Telex: 24454)

West London Auctions, Sandringham Mews, High Street, Ealing, London W5 (Tel: 01-567 6215/7096)

English Counties

Baker Donnelly, The Romsey Auction Rooms, 86 The Hundred, Romsey, Hampshire SO5 8DG (Tel: Romsey 513331)

Boardman, Fine Art Auctioneers, Station Road Corner, Haverhill, Suffolk (Tel: Haverhill 3784)

Buckell & Ballard, 49 Parsons Street, Banbury, Oxon OX16 8PF (Tel: Banbury 53191)

Button, Menhenitt & Mutton Ltd, Belmont Auction Rooms, Wadebridge, Cornwall (Tel: Wadebridge 2059)

Cavendish House (Cheltenham) Ltd, Cambray Auction Galleries, 26 Cambray Place, Cheltenham, Gloucestershire (Tel: Cheltenham 24679)

Crewkerne Salerooms, 19B Market Street, Crewkerne, Somerset (Tel: Crewkerne 2403)

Dacre, Son & Hartley, 1/5 The Grove, Ilkley, W. Yorkshire (Tel: Ilkley 600655)

Dreweatt, Watson & Barton, Market Place, Newbury, Berkshire (Tel: Newbury 46000 Telex: 848580)

Frank H. Fellows & Sons, Bedford House, 88 Hagley Road, Edgbaston, Birmingham (Tel: 021-454 1261/1219)

Garrod, Turner, Fine Art Department, 50 St Nicholas Street,

Ipswich, Suffolk (Tel: Ipswich 54664/53114/6)

Geering & Colyer, Highgate, Hawkhurst, Kent (Tel: Hawkhurst 3181); Sales at The Spa Hotel, Tunbridge Wells, Kent (Tel: Tunbridge Wells 20331; Telex: Spa Hotel 957188)

Jackson-Stops & Staff, High Street, Chipping Campden, Gloucestershire (Tel: Evesham 840224)

Laidlaws, Crown Court Auction Mart, off Wood Street, Wakefield, Yorkshire WF1 2SU (Tel: Wakefield 75301)

W.H. Lane & Son, Central Auction Rooms, Penzance, Cornwall TR18 2QT (Tel: Penzance 2286/9; Tgms: Lane Penzance)

Locke and England, 1 & 2 Euston Place, Leamington Spa, Warwickshire (Tel: Leamington Spa 27988)

May, Whetter & Grose, Cornubia Hall, Par, Cornwall (Tel: Par 2271)

Messenger May Baverstock, 93 High Street, Godalming, Surrey (Tel: Godalming 23567/8)

Outhwaite & Litherland, Kingsway Galleries, Fontenoy Street, Liverpool L3 2BE (Tel: 051-236 6561)

Parsons Welch & Cowell, 129 High Street, Sevenoaks, Kent (Tel: Sevenoaks 51211/4)

Pearson's, 99 & 293 Fleet Road, Fleet, Hampshire (Tel: Fleet 3166)

Phillips in Knowle, The Old House, Station Road, Knowle, Solihull, W. Midlands (Tel: Knowle 6151)

Phillips at Hepper House, 17a East Parade, Leeds, W. Yorkshire LS1 2BU (Tel: Leeds 40029/30192)

Phillips & Jollys, Auction Rooms of Bath, 1 Old King Street, Bath, Avon (Tel: Bath 310609/310709)

Sotheby Bearne, Rainbow, Avenue Road, Torquay, Devon TQ2 5TG (Tel: Torquay 26277; Telex: 42661)

Sotheby Humberts, Magdalene House, Magdalene Street, Taunton, Somerset (Tel: Taunton 88441)

Sotheby King & Chasemore, Station Road, Pulborough, Sussex (Tel: Pulborough 2081/6)

Spear & Sons, Wickham Market Sale Rooms, Nr Woodbridge, Suffolk IP13 0QX (Tel: Woodbridge 746323 — Monday only).

Henry Spencer & Sons, Fine Art Auctioneers, 20 The Square, Retford Nottinghamshire DN22 6DJ (Tel: Retford 706767)

Stride & Son, Southdown House Salerooms, St John's Street, Chichester, Sussex (Tel: Chichester 82626)

Vidler & Co, Rye Auction Galleries, Cinque Ports Street, Rye, E. Sussex (Tel: Rye 2124/5)

Vost's, East Wing, Layer Marney Tower, Nr Colchester, Essex

(Tel: Colchester 330250)

Wallis & Wallis, Regency House, 1 Albion Street, Lewes, Sussex (Tel: Lewes 3137; Tgms: Wallauct Lewes; Telex: 896691 TLX1RG; Salerooms: Cliffe Hall)

Wellar Eggar, Castle Showrooms, Farnham, Surrey (Tel: Farnham 6221)

Weller & Dufty Ltd, The Fine Art Salerooms, 141 Bromsgrove Street, Birmingham, W. Midlands B5 6RQ

Woolley & Wallis, The Castle Auction Mart, Castle Street, Salisbury (Tel: Salisbury 27405)

Norman Wright and Partners, 26 Priestgate, Peterborough, Northamptonshire (Tel: Peterborough 67361)

Scotland

Christie's & Edmiston's, 164/166 Bath Street, Glasgow G2 4TG (Tel: 041-332 8134)

Lyon & Turnbull Ltd, 51 George Street, Edinburgh EH2 2HT (Tel: 031-225 4627)

Phillips in Scotland, 65 George Street, Edinburgh EH2 2JL (Tel: 031-225 2266; Tgms: Phillips Edinburgh)

Phillips in Scotland, 98 Sauchiehall Street, Glasgow G2 2DQ (Tel: 041-332 3386)

Organisers of fairs

Bedfordshire

Mrs Jean Tibbles, 66 Barford Road, Blunham, Bedfordshire (Tel: Biggleswade 40190)

Luton Antiques Fairs, 61 Cheshford Road, Luton, Bedfordshire (Tel: Luton 25546)

Berkshire

Granny's Attic Antique Fairs, 'Wisteria', The Grange, Grange Lane, Cookham, Nr Maidenhead, Berkshire. (Tel: Bourne End 23080); 'Hethersett', Harcourt Road, Dorney Reach, Nr Maidenhead, Berkshire. (Tel: Maidenhead 26619)

Mrs M. O'Neill, 40 Dedworth Road, Windsor, Berkshire (Tel: Windsor 54665)

Buckinghamshire
Mrs S. Vallance, Turpin's Ride, Amersham Road, Chalfont St. Giles, Buckinghamshire (Tel: Chalfont St. Giles 4083)

Cambridgeshire
Herridge's Fairs, Rathmore House, Sutton, Ely, Cambridgeshire (Tel: Ely 778356)

Cheshire
Stancie Cutler, Nantwich Civic Hall, Nantwich, Cheshire (Tel: Nantwich 584736)

Derbyshire
Whatnot Fairs, Antiques Coffee House, Buxton Road, Bakewell, Derbyshire (Tel: Bakewell 3544)

Devon
West Country Antiques & Collectors Fairs, 11 Boutport Street, Barnstaple, Devon (Tel: Barnstaple 3641)

Dorset
L. Saunders Fairs, PO Box 30, Bournemouth, Dorset (Tel: Bournemouth 24291)
New Forest Antique Fairs, 76 Uplands Road, West Moors, Wimborne, Dorset (Tel:Ferndown 873993)

Essex
Mrs C. Hurst, 106 Queens Road, Buckhurst Hill, Essex (Tel: 01-504 2666)

Gloucestershire
Five Star Antique Fairs, 88 Insley Gardens, Hucclecote, Gloucester (Tel Gloucester 64503)
Mary Packham Antiques Fairs, 7 Royal Well Place, Cheltenham, Gloucestershire (Tel: Cheltenham 513485)

Hampshire
Magpie Fayres, 9 King's Saltern Road, Lymington, Hampshire (Tel: Lymington 73549)

Hertfordshire
Chiltern Fairs, The Gables, Berks Hill, Chorleywood, Hertfordshire (Tel: Chorleywood 2144)

Lima Antiques, North House, 8 Danesbury Park Road, Old Welwyn, Hertfordshire (Tel: Welwyn 4744)

Lancashire
Philip Nevitsky, 191 Manchester Road, Rochdale, Lancashire (Tel: Rochdale 58266)

Leicestershire
Bob Evans, Quaintree, Kirby Bellars, Melton Mowbray, Leicestershire (Tel: Melton Mowbray 812627)

Lincolnshire
Rutland Antiques, 32a St. Peter's Street, Stamford, Lincolnshire (Tel: Stamford 51188 (day) 54489 (24 hrs.))

London
Antiquarian Booksellers Association, 154 Buckingham Palace Road, London SW1 (Tel: 01-730 9273)
Arms Fairs Ltd, 40 Great James Street, London WC1N 3HB (Tel: 01-405 7933)
Heritage Antiques Fairs, PO Box 149, London W9 1QN (Tel: 01-624 5173 (day)/01-624 1787 (evg.))
Johanna Harrison Associates, 14 Sydney House, Woodstock Road, London W4 (Tel: 01-994 7430)
Step-in Markets, 105 Warwick Road, London SW5 (Tel: 01-370 1267)

Manchester
Unicorn Antique & Collectors Fairs, 21 Craigwell Road, Prestwich, Manchester (Tel: 061-740 4277)

Middlesex
Barbara Adams, 49 Maryland Way, Sunbury-on-Thames, Middlesex (Tel: Sunbury-on-Thames 84587)
Pickwick Fairs, 1 Gaston Way, Shepperton, Middlesex (Tel: Walton-on-Thames 29144)

Oxfordshire
Portcullis Fairs, 6 St Peter's Street, Wallingford, Oxon (Tel: Wallingford 39345)

Shropshire
Antiques in Britain Fairs, Hopton Castle, Craven Arms, Salop

(Tel: Bucknell 356)
Middleton Fairs, 15 Hollybush Road, Bridgnorth, Salop (Tel: Bridgnorth 4114)

Staffordshire
West Midland Antiques Fairs, Regent House, St Lawrence Way, Gnosall, Stafford (Tel: Stafford 823014)

Surrey
Antiques & Collectors Club, No. 1 Warehouse, Horley Row, Horley, Surrey (Tel: Horley 72206)
Joan Braganza, 47 Deerings Road, Reigate, Surrey (Tel: Reigate 45587)

Sussex
Christopher Ann, Drusillas, Alfriston, Sussex (Tel: Alfriston 870234/870656)
Penman Antiques Fairs, Cockhaise Mill, Monteswood Lane, Haywards Heath, Sussex (Tel: Lindfield 2514)

Yorkshire
Bowman Fairs, 7 Church Hill, Bramhope, Leeds LS16 9BA (Tel: Leeds 843333)
Castle Fairs, Castle Gate, York (Tel: York 27222)

Trade services and suppliers

London
And So To Bed Ltd, 7 New King's Road, London SW6 (Tel: 01-731 3593/4). Service: Renovation of brass bedsteads
Anglo-Persian Carpet Co Ltd, The Arcade, South Kensington Station, London SW7 (Tel: 01-589 5457). Service: Hand cleaning, repairs, valuations of antique and contemporary oriental carpets.
Antique Restorations, 211 Westbourne Park Road, London W11 (Tel: 01-727 0467). Service: Repair and restoration of painted and decorated furniture, oriental lacquer and japanning, carving and gilding.

Benardout & Benardout, 7 Thurloe Place, London SW7 (Tel: 01-584 7658). Service: Cleaning, restoration, valuations of carpets and rugs.

Aubrey Brocklehurst, 124 Cromwell Road, London SW7 (Tel: 01-373 0319). Service: Restoration and repair of clocks, barometers and small items of furniture.

Chelsea Bric-à-Brac Shop Ltd, 16 Hartfield Road, Wimbledon, London SW19 (Tel: 01-946 6894). Service: Repairs to furniture and iron and brass.

Chinamend Ltd, 54 Walton Street, London SW3 (Tel: 01-589 1182). Service: Restoration of china, porcelain and pottery.

Dolphin Antiques, 2b Englands Lane, Hampstead, London NW3 (Tel: 01-722 7003). Service: Restoration of furniture, cabinetwork, gilding, leathering boulle and marquetry or decorated furniture.

Fagin's Phonograph Emporium, 189 Blackstock Road, London N5 (Tel: 01-359 4793/3159). Service: Spares for vintage talking machines (phonographs, gramophones, etc) and restoration.

Paul Ferguson - Woodcarver/Gilder, Workshop 5, 1st Floor, 38 Mount Pleasant, London WC1. (Tel: 01-278 8759). Service: Picture frames carved and gilded, frames enlarged/reduced; carving repairs and restoration of antiques and works of art.

The Golden Past, 6 Brook Street, London W1 (Tel: 01-493 6422). Service: Repairs, valuation to clients' antique jewellery and silver.

Stephen Morris Shipping, 89 Upper Street (Offices), London N1 (Tel: 01-359 3159; Telex: 261707). Service: Specialist packers and shippers of antiques and bric-à-brac. Services include collections, pre-packing, warehousing, container loading and insurance.

Picreator Enterprises Ltd, 44 Park View Gardens, Hendon, London NW4 (Tel: 01-202 8972). Service: Mail order range of professional conservation/restoration materials.

H.W. Poulter & Son, 279 Fulham Road, London SW10 (Tel: 01-352 7268). Service: Restoration and repairs to marble and sculptures, etc.

L.J. Roberton Ltd, 98-122 Green Street, Forest Gate, London E7 (Tel: 01-552 1132). Service: Full export packing, documentation and shipping service worldwide. Courier available upon request.

The Sladmore Gallery, 32 Bruton Place, London W1 (Tel: 01-499 0365). Service: Valuations, cleaning and restoring bronze sculpture.

Christopher Wray's Lighting Emporium, 600 King's Road, London SW6 (Tel: 01-736 8434). Service: Replacement parts for oil and gas lamps, glass shades, chimneys, galleries, burners, etc.

Avon
Bibliotique, 2 Canton Place, London Road, Bath (Tel: Bath 312932). Service: Bookbinding.

Berkshire
Nell Gwyn's House, 5 Church Street, Windsor (Tel: Windsor 66246). Service: Silver plate resilvered.
Times Past Antiques Ltd, 59 High Street, Eton (Tel: Windsor 57018). Service: Antique clock repairs.

Cambridgeshire
Ernest Hilton Ltd, 33 Trumpington Street, Cambridge (Tel: Cambridge 61529). Service: Valuations, restorations, framing of oils, watercolours, drawings and prints.

Cheshire
Cranford Galleries, 10 King Street, Knutsford (Tel: Knutsford 3646). Service: Picture framing and mounting.

Cornwall
Amamus Ltd, Country Antiques, Fore Street, Grampound, Nr. Truro (Tel: Grampound Road 882009). Service: Pine stripping.

Cumbria
Windermere & Bowness Dollmaking Co, College Road, Windermere (Tel: Windermere 4785). Service: Restoration and re-dressing of antique dolls; new dolls made.

Dorset
J.L. Arditti, 88 Bargates, Christchurch (Tel: Christchurch 485414). Service: Repairs and cleaning of old Persian rugs.
Lorna M. Maund, Sheraton House, Oakwood Road, Highcliffe, Christchurch (Tel: Highcliffe 5033). Service: Colouring of antique maps, plans and sea charts.

Gloucestershire
Keith Bawden, Furniture Restorer, Mews Workshops, Montpellier Retreat, Cheltenham (Tel: Cheltenham 30320). Service:

Restoration, polishing, waxing, fitting of leathers to desks, upholstery, rush seating and caning.

David Slade, 45 Leckhampton Road, Cheltenham (Tel: Cheltenham 519598). Service: Cleaning, restoring, colouring, mounting of antique prints.

Thornborough Galleries, 28 Gloucester Street, Cirencester (Tel: Cirencester 2055). Service: Cleaning, restoration and valuation of old Oriental carpets.

Hampshire

Robert Alexander, 11 King's Road, Fleet (Tel: Fleet 3713). Service: Antique furniture restoration.

David Hallett Antiques, 50a Stockbridge Road, Winchester (Tel: Winchester 3121). Service: Restoration and upholstery of antiques, tooled leather desk tops.

Hertfordshire

Neale Antiques, 21 Old Cross, Hertford (Tel: Hertford 52519). Service: Repairs and replating antique and modern silver, valuations; repairs to gold and silver jewellery.

Kent

Adlam Burnett, Finchcocks, Goudhurst (Tel: Goudhurst 211702). Service: Restoration of antique keyboard musical instruments.

Nigel Coleman, High Street, Brasted (Tel: Westerham 64042). Service: Barometer restoration.

Lancashire

Gallery 77, 18 Princess Street, Bradshawgate, Bolton (Tel: Bolton 35252). Service: Picture framers and restorers, oils and watercolours.

Swag, 24-26 Leyland Road, Penwortham, Preston (Tel: Preston 744970). Service: Repairs, restoration and dressing service for old dolls.

Merseyside

Hoylake Antiques, 23 Grove Road, Hoylake, Wirral (Tel: 051-632 1888). Service: Antique clocks and jewellery repaired and restored.

Norfolk

The Old Granary Studio, Kings Staithe Lane, Kings Lynn (Tel:

Kings Lynn 5509). Service: Picture framing, restoration, heat-sealing, block-mounting, gilding, mount-cutting.

Northamptonshire
Finedon Antiques Centre, 3 Church Street, Finedon (Tel: Wellingborough 680316/680430). Service: Furniture restoration, metal cleaning and polishing, watch and clock repairs, furniture stripping, upholstery, valuations.

Oxfordshire
Barry M. Keene Gallery, Queens Hall, 2 Greys Road, Henley on Thames (Tel: Henley 77119). Service: Picture framing and restoration.

Staffordshire
The Tinder Box Antiques, 136a Bucknall New Road, Hanley, Stoke-on-Trent (Tel: Stoke-on-Trent 550508) Service: Complete renewal of oil lamps, parts, etc., handpainted porcelain undertaken, Victorian brass cleaned and buffed.

Suffolk
Clare Renovation, 4 Market Hill, Clare, Sudbury (Tel: Clare 405). Service: Restoration and polishing, reupholstery, chairs recaned and rerushed.
David & Dorothy Lee, 21 High Street, Southwold (Tel: Southwold 722795). Service: Restoration and repair of furniture.

Surrey
Casque & Gauntlet Antiques Ltd, 55-59 Badshot Lea Road, Badshot Lea, Nr. Farnham (Tel: Aldershot 20745). Service: Refurbishing of antique arms and armour.

Sussex
John Cowderoy Antiques, 42 South Street, Eastbourne (Tel: Eastbourne 20058). Service: Antique clock and musical box restoration.
David Fileman Antiques, Squirrels, Bayards, Steyning (Tel: Steyning 813229). Service: Restoration of antique glass, chandeliers, candelabra, also cleaning.

Warwickshire
Warwick Antiques, 16-18 High Street, Warwick (Tel: Warwick

42482). Service: Metalware restoration.

West Midlands
Meriden House Antiques, Meriden House, Market Street, Stourbridge (Tel: Stourbridge 5384). Service: Restoration of furniture and dolls.

Wiltshire
Winstanley Bookbinders, 213 Devizes Road, Salisbury (Tel: Salisbury 4998). Service: Antiquarian books restored, selected limited edition binding, ancillary artwork service.

Yorkshire
J.H. Cooper & Son (Ilkley) Ltd, 31-35 Church Street and 50 Leeds Road, Ilkley (Tel: Ilkley 608020/608942). Service: Restoration of antique furniture and works of art.

Bibliography

Andrews, John, *The Price Guide to Antique Furniture,* Antique Collectors' Club, 2nd ed 1978

Arwas, Victor, *Glass - Art Nouveau to Art Deco,* Academy Editions 1978

Austin, Brian, *A Handbook of Styles in English Antique Furniture,* W. Foulsham 1974

Bannister, Judith (ed), *English Silver Hall Marks,* W. Foulsham 1970

Beeching, Wilfred A., *Century of the Typewriter,* Heinemann 1974

Bradbury, Frederick, *Bradbury's Book of Hallmarks,* J. W. Northend 1927; revised 1976

Camerer Cuss, T.P., *The Camerer Cuss Book of Antique Watches,* Antique Collectors' Club 1976

Cameron, Ian; Kingsley Rowe, Elizabeth; Tunikowska, Halina; Fagg, Christopher; Tayler, Bettina (eds), *The Collector's Encyclopaedia: Victoriana to Art Deco,* Collins 1974

Catley, Bryan, *Art Deco and Other Figures,* Antique Collectors' Club 1978

Cooper, Jeremy, *The Complete Guide to London's Antique Markets,* Thames & Hudson 1974

Coysh, A.W., *The Antique Buyer's Dictionary of Names,* David & Charles 1970; Pan 1972

Criswell, Grover C., *Confederate and Southern State Bonds,* Criswell's (USA) 1961; 2nd ed 1979; revised 1980

Dempsey, Mike (ed), *Bubbles: Early Advertising Art from A & F Pears Ltd,* Fontana 1978

Divis, Jan, *Silver Marks of the World,* Hamlyn 1976

Douglas, Jane, *Collectable Things,* Countrywise Books 1961

Drumm, U. and Henseler, A., *Chinesische Anleihen und Aktien,* Freunde Historische Wertpapiere (Germany) 1976

Drumm, U. and Henseler, A., *Old Securities, Russian Railway Bonds,* Freunde Historische Wertpapiere (Germany) 1975; 2nd ed 1979

Fisher, Stanley W., *British Pottery and Porcelain,* Arco Publications 1962

Flick, Pauline, *Discovering Toys and Toy Museums,* Shire Publications 1971

Gernsheim, Helmut and Gernsheim, Alison, *The History of Photography: from the earliest use of camera obscura in the 11th century up to 1914,* Oxford University Press (New York) 1955; McGraw-Hill (New York) revised 1969

Gernsheim, Helmut and Gernsheim, Alison, *Masterpieces of Victorian*

Photography, Phaidon 1951

Godden, Geoffrey A., *Coalport and Coalbrookdale Porcelains,* Herbert Jenkins 1970

Godden, G.A. *Encyclopaedia of British Pottery and Porcelain Marks,* Jenkins 1964

Hendy, Robin, *Collecting Old Bonds and Shares,* Stanley Gibbons 1978

Howarth-Loomes, B.E.C., *Victorian Photography, A Collector's Guide,* Ward Lock 1974

Hughes, G. Bernard, *Collecting Antiques,* Country Life, revised ed 1960

Hughes, G. Bernard, *The Country Life Collector's Pocket Book of China,* Country Life 1965; revised ed 1977

Jackson, Radway, *English Pewter Touchmarks,* W. Foulsham 1970

Jewell, Brian, *Collecting for Tomorrow,* Blandford Press 1979

Kennedy, Carol, *Buying Antiques in Europe: What to Buy and Where,* Bowker 1976

Kennedy, Richard (illus.) *The Garden of the Night,* The Whittington Press 1979

Kennedy, Richard (illus.) *The Song of Songs,* The Whittington Press 1976

Kershaw, Peter, *A Beginner's Guide to Auctions,* Rapp & Whiting 1968

Litherland, G. (ed), *Antique Glass Bottles: an illustrated price guide,* Midlands Antique Bottle Publishing 1977; Southern Collectors Publications, revised 1979

Litherland, G. (ed), *Bottle Collecting with Price Guide,* MAB Publishing 1978; Southern Collectors Publications, revised 1979

Luecke, Marjorie Ann, *The International Antiques Market: A Guide for Investors and Collectors,* A.S. Barnes & Co. Inc. (USA) 1979

Mackay, James, *Collectables,* Macdonald & Jane's 1979

Mackay, James, *A Dictionary of Small Antiques,* Ward Lock 1975

McClelland, Nancy and Rennert, Jack (eds), *A Century of Posters,* Phillips (New York) 1979

Mountfield, David, *The Antique Collector's Illustrated Dictionary,* Hamlyn 1974

Narbeth, Colin; Hendy, Robin; Stocker, Christopher, *Collecting Paper Money and Bonds,* Cassell 1979

Negus, Arthur, *Going for a Song: English Furniture — Arthur Negus talks to Max Robertson,* BBC 1969

Osborne, Harold (ed), *The Oxford Companion to the Decorative Arts,* Oxford University Press 1975

Pearsall, Ronald, *Collecting Mechanical Antiques,* David & Charles 1973

Pine, Nicholas, *Goss China Arms, Decorations and their Values* Milestone Publications 1979

Rowe, F. Gordon, *The Georgian Child,* Phoenix House 1961

Rowe, F. Gordon, *Home Furnishing with Antiques*, Abbey Fine Arts 1969

Rowe, F. Gordon, *The Victorian Child*, Phoenix House 1959

Smith, Alan (ed), *The Country Life International Dictionary of Clocks*, Country Life 1979

Stammers, M.K., *Discovering Maritime Museums and Historic Ships*, Shire Publications 1979

Stanton, Carol Ann, *Heubach's Little Characters, Dolls and Figurines 1850-1930*, Living Dolls Publications 1978

Toller, Jane, *Country Furniture*, David & Charles 1973

Toulson, Shirley, *Discovering Farm Parks and Farm Museums*, Shire Publications 1977

Whittington, Peter, *Undiscovered Antiques*, Garnstone Press 1972

Wills, Geoffrey, *The Country Life Collector's Pocket Book of Glass*, Country Life 1966; revised 1979

Witkin, Lee D. and London, Barbara, *The Photograph Collector's Guide*, Secker & Warburg 1979

Wood, Christopher, *The Dictionary of Victorian Painters*, Antique Collectors' Club 1971; revised 1978

Annual Publications

Arts Review Yearbook, ed. Annabel Terry-Engel, Eaton House

The British Art & Antiques Yearbook, ed. Marcelle d'Argy Smith, National Magazine Company

The International Antiques Yearbook, compiled by Marcelle d'Argy Smith and Elizabeth Dick, National Magazine Company

The Libraries, Museums and Art Galleries Yearbook, James Clarke.

The Lyle Official Antiques Review, ed. Tony Curtis, Lyle Publications

Museums and Art Galleries in the North of England, North of England Museums Service

Museums and Galleries in Great Britain and Ireland, ABC Publications

The Museums Yearbook, Museums Association

The Register of Defunct and Other Companies, Removed from the Stock Exchange Official Yearbook, ed. Jeffrey Russell Knight, Thomas Skinner

Stately Homes, Museums and Gardens in Great Britain, Automobile Association

Index